HOW TO READ

HOW
TO
READ

THE EGYPTIAN
BOOK OF THE DEAD

BARRY KEMP

W. W. NORTON & COMPANY
New York · London

First published in Great Britain by Granta Publications

For information about permission to reproduce selections from this book,
write to Permissions, W. W. Norton & Company, Inc.
500 Fifth Avenue, New York, NY 10110

For information about special discounts for bulk purchases, please contact
W. W. Norton Special Sales at specialsales@wwnorton.com or 800-233-4830

Manufacturing by Courier Westford
Production manager: Devon Zahn

Library of Congress Cataloging-in-Publication Data

Kemp, Barry J.
How to read the Egyptian Book of the dead / Barry Kemp. — 1st American ed.
      p. cm. — (How to read)
Includes bibliographical references and index.
ISBN 978-0-393-33079-3 (pbk.)
1. Book of the dead. 2. Incantations, Egyptian. 3. Future life. I. Title
PJ1557.K46 2008
299′.3123—dc22
2008019191

W. W. Norton & Company, Inc.
500 Fifth Avenue, New York, N.Y. 10110
www.wwnorton.com

W. W. Norton & Company Ltd.
Castle House, 75/76 Wells Street, London W1T 3QT

1 2 3 4 5 6 7 8 9 0

CONTENTS

How am I to read *How to Read*?

This series is based on a very simple, but novel idea. Most beginners' guides to great thinkers and writers offer either potted biographies or condensed summaries of their major works, or perhaps even both. *How to Read*, by contrast, brings the reader face-to-face with the writing itself in the company of an expert guide. Its starting point is that in order to get close to what a writer is all about, you have to get close to the words they actually use and be shown how to read those words.

Every book in the series is in a way a masterclass in reading. Each author has selected ten or so short extracts from a writer's work and looks at them in detail as a way of revealing their central ideas and thereby opening doors on to a whole world of thought. Sometimes these extracts are arranged chronologically to give a sense of a thinker's development over time, sometimes not. The books are not merely compilations of a thinker's most famous passages, their 'greatest hits', but rather they offer a series of clues or keys that will enable readers to go on and make discoveries of their own. In addition to the texts and readings, each book provides a short biographical chronology and suggestions for further reading, Internet resources, and so on. The books in the *How to Read* series don't claim to tell you all you need to know about Freud, Nietzsche and Darwin, or indeed Shakespeare and the Marquis de Sade, but they do offer the best starting point for further exploration.

Unlike the available second-hand versions of the minds that have shaped our intellectual, cultural, religious, political and scientific landscape, *How to Read* offers a refreshing set of first-hand encounters with those minds. Our hope is that these books will, by turn, instruct, intrigue, embolden, encourage and delight.

Simon Critchley
New School for Social Research, New York

ACKNOWLEDGEMENTS

The invitation from George Miller to write this book, and so to confront a text I have long avoided, was too tempting to turn down. I have learned much and put my thoughts into better order. Bella Shand has been a model editor. I'd also like to thank the Templeton Foundation for their grant for research into ancient Egyptian spirituality.

A NOTE ON TRANSLATION

The translation I have mostly used is that of R. O. Faulkner, *The Ancient Egyptian Book of the Dead* (London, British Museum Press, 1985), although on occasion I have preferred the turns of phrase in the translation by T. G. Allen, *The Book of the Dead or Going Forth by Day; ideas of the ancient Egyptians concerning the Hereafter as expressed in their own terms* (Chicago, University of Chicago Press, 1974). The original texts were mostly written in black ink except for the headings to spells and certain other kinds of ancient editorial matter, which were written in red. I have followed the convention of italicizing red-ink passages. Ancient Egyptian was written as continuous text, without breaks or punctuation. Modern translations are bound to introduce both, but in doing so impose another set of translator's judgements.

INTRODUCTION

In the 1999 Hollywood film *The Mummy*, two rival groups of treasure-hunters discover the Book of the Dead in an Egyptian city lost in the desert. As they find out to their cost, its purpose is to bring the dead back to life, but not in their original pristine form. The plot centres on the attempts by the (accidentally) revivified priest Imhotep to regain his original appearance by absorbing the body parts, including the blood, of the living. The cast of characters is steadily diminished as Imhotep kills them off one by one.

The film never claimed historical authenticity but did present, albeit skewed, some of the key themes found in the ancient Egyptian Book of the Dead. No living person expected literally to resurrect from the dead, but the ancient Egyptians did believe their physical bodies would be renewed in the spiritual realm of the 'Otherworld', their name for the afterlife. The real, ancient Egyptian Book of the Dead was a collection of 'spells' that prepared the Egyptians for life after death and which had the power to conjure up all the parts of one's body for the spiritual journey.

The Otherworld was not a place of earthly pleasures or of family reunions. Unlike in Greek mythology, where Greeks might meet old friends and figures from history wandering on the Elysian fields, the Otherworld was a state of spiritual existence in which an individual would at moments merge with

godheads: with Ra, who combined the solar source of life;
with Osiris, who triumphed over the corruptions of the flesh
and the assaults of evil forces; with Atum, the creative force
that originally gave the universe its shape. This existence had
a sense of place and physicality realized in some detail. Its
gods, demons, mysterious locations and potential obstacles,
which the dead individual faced alone, lent it a threatening
aspect. The Book of the Dead, by means of its spells, con-
ferred on the owner the power to navigate successfully – for
eternity – through its various realms.

The Mummy exploits the mystique that surrounds popular
perceptions of ancient Egypt, a world of overbearing architecture and religious images, partly set in dark underground
treasure-filled catacombs, served by eerie, shaven priests. Much
modern writing about ancient Egypt for the general public is at
pains to correct this image and to show that the Egyptians were
actually very human, lived family lives in normal houses and
enjoyed picnic parties in the countryside. They wrote stories,
love poems and touching hymns of personal piety, all of which
can be read straightforwardly in translation. These Egyptians are
people we can engage with without too much difficulty.

These approachable and comprehensible Egyptians –
weren't they just like us? – are also the same people who read
the Book of the Dead. And reading the Book of the Dead, we
are presented with a third, alternative, view of the ancient
Egyptians. The Book of the Dead opens up their minds to us,
and an unfamiliar picture emerges. It reveals a way of expression and thinking that is hard for us to engage with. Yet if we
want to get to know the Egyptians as they really were, then
we have to enter their minds and try, at least a little, to com-
prehend the wider world that they thought they occupied.
They were like us, but only so far.

The difference is more profound than their mass of gods and fragments of unfamiliar mythology. The Book of the Dead (and some of its companion texts) reveals a relationship between the human individual and the divine which is quite unlike that found in some of the major religions of the modern world (especially Christianity and Islam). It also exemplifies a frustrating characteristic of the ancient Egyptian mind (from our point of view), a wide tolerance of what, to us, is an inconsistent spiritual landscape. The Egyptians seem to have comprehended their world of spiritual forces as a series of fragments. In their minds it was not necessary to unify the fragments into a single theological scheme. Beliefs stated in parallel to one another had equal validity, and it was the point of view of the moment that gave authority to a statement. Several basic themes were held in mind at the same time, and ancient Egyptians would switch from one to another. The Book of the Dead constantly moves its points of reference, although its shifting perspectives were within quite restricted limits, set by an adherence to traditions. Christianity and Islam early on emphasized teaching and guidance for believers, and this has remained a marked characteristic of both. In comparison the Egyptians appreciated their religious texts intuitively, as part of their culture, and found little need for exposition, for there was no division between believers and non-believers. It is this and the greater cultural gap that often leaves us floundering to find explanations and interpretations of their beliefs.

The makers of *The Mummy* decided that something called a 'Book' should look like a book as we understand the term, and produced a thick, heavy object whose few pages were hinged plates of an almost black metal. It could be opened only by rotating a star-shaped metal 'key' engraved with a scarab beetle. 'Book' is an English translation of a word in ancient Egyptian that in fact refers to an extensive piece of writing of serious philosophical intent. That writing was mostly done on a roll of papyrus, an early equivalent of paper made from thin slices of the thick fibrous stems of the papyrus plant glued together to form a continuous sheet. Many surviving copies of the Book of the Dead were written on papyrus. A few were on leather and more were on linen. It was also copied on to coffins and the walls of the tomb, and individual spells found their way on to amulets or figurines. Its language was ancient Egyptian, written for a time with pen and ink in a semi-cursive form of hieroglyphic writing. Later came the swifter style of fully developed flowing handwriting (hieratic), followed even later by an abbreviated derivative version (demotic). It can mostly be translated reliably although often we cannot be sure of the precise nuance of individual words.

Over the centuries thousands of copies were produced. It was not a secret text, although it required study and the mastery of a technical vocabulary.[1] A few of its spells demand that the owner or reader not pass the spell on to anyone else, but this exemplifies the intensely private world that the Book sought to create, in which the reader, facing the Otherworld alone, excludes all consideration of normal human existence. The Book of the Dead was available for purchase at different lengths, with different selections of spells, and with cheap or expensive styles of illustration. They could reach 41 metres in length (the Greenfield Papyrus in the British Museum). The best were works of art. A copy could be bought for the equivalent of the price of a bed, or the more sumptuously illustrated for the price of an ox. There was probably nothing to stop a person from borrowing one from someone else and copying it out. In all likelihood, however, temple libraries were the places where the majority of master copies were kept and where learned men from time to time added fresh spells. Most Books of the Dead were owned by men, and the texts were certainly written on that assumption, but examples made for women are known, too.

The collection of spells that became the Book of the Dead began to take shape, as far as we know, not long before the beginning of the New Kingdom (c. 1550 BC). This was the third major period of ancient Egyptian history that was marked by the acquisition of empire and great prosperity, and had been preceded two centuries before by a Middle Kingdom and, before that, by an Old Kingdom, the age of pyramid building. By the time of the New Kingdom ancient Egyptian civilization – its beginnings detectable around 3000 BC – had reached a mature stage of development. Many of the Book's spells were based on much earlier versions, written on the insides of coffins (the Coffin Texts) or, in an even earlier age, that of the Old Kingdom, on the inside walls of the chambers of some of the pyramids. The earliest of these, the pyramid of King Unas, dates to about 2345 BC. One study has estimated that, of the 192 numbered spells of the Book of the Dead, all but 79 have a background in the Coffin Texts which had been created at least five centuries earlier.

There is no world census of how many copies exist out of the ground (although one is in progress), but one might guess at a figure in the low thousands (not counting individual spells on small religious objects).[2] The British Museum has at least twenty-four, the Oriental Institute of Chicago Museum eleven, the Louvre over seventy, the Vatican at least fourteen. The Mormon Church counts fragments of two (The Joseph Smith papyri) amongst its founding documents.[3]

Books of the Dead were part of early collections of antiquities from Egypt made before hieroglyphs could be translated, which only happened after the decipherment of hieroglyphic writing in the 1820s and '30s. The first full published translation, in German, was that of Carl Richard Lepsius in 1842. The title of his book, *Das Todtenbuch der Ägypter* (The Book of the Dead of the Egyptians), gave authority to this name, even though the Egyptians themselves called it the 'Coming Forth by Day'. The contents of the Book became known to the interested public, at least of the West, in the latter part of the nineteenth century. In the English-speaking world dissemination was aided by an edition with an extensive introduction by E. A. Wallis Budge of the British Museum. Its hold has been such that reprints continue to be made.

Because there is no significant living group of people that holds Osiris, Ra and Atum to be true gods, ancient Egyptian religion has no theologians or saintly practitioners. Study of the Book of the Dead thus lacks the explanatory and devotional literature that people otherwise expect when taking a serious interest in a religion. The modern world views Egyptian religion from an external perspective, as an interesting if difficult aspect of another society's culture, one that is long dead. At its most intensive and professional, within Egyptology, study of the Book of the Dead typically charts how individual spells have been transmitted, and correlates mythological details that are also to be found in other Egyptian religious sources. Comments on its content have often been disapproving, dwelling on the way that constant copying of the texts introduced mistakes and a presumed decline in understanding, and on what has been perceived as an inadequate measure of social conscience when compared especially with Christianity. The spells that wipe out past wrongdoing in the Otherworld's hall of judgement have particularly brought adverse comment because in place of confession comes detailed denial of personal wrongdoing and thus a rejection of guilt.

As in *The Mummy*, using the Book successfully involves 'speaking' the spells, and 'knowing' their content. Each one begins with the heading 'Spell for . . .'. The word translated 'spell' means both 'mouth' and the speech that comes from it. Alternative translations are 'chapter' or 'utterance'. Sometimes speaking the words is enough to cast the spell; sometimes they are reinforced by speaking them over a carefully described object, such as a 'scarab made from nephrite, mounted in fine gold, with a ring of silver, and placed at the throat of the deceased' (Spell 30). The 'voice' in the Book of the Dead is often in the first person. Sometimes, however, the text required the name of the owner to be inserted. A common modern convention is to substitute for the personal name the capital letter N. I have chosen to use the word 'reader' instead to encourage a sense of engagement.

The translation 'spell' is justified because within the texts words are uttered to achieve a particular result, and the Egyptian concept of 'magic' is never far away. Spell 90, for example (quoted at the head of Chapter 1), guards against a demon stealing the power to voice the magic that lies within the reader. The reason that some scholars prefer the translation 'Chapter' is that many of the texts contain long digressions which acquaint the reader with ancient Egyptian mythological knowledge. This is the 'knowing' aspect of the spells. From the Book of the Dead the reader acquired a picture of the Otherworld as a series of snapshots that, when taken together, built up into a world that has been imagined in some detail, although not in a topographic style that makes explicit links. The reader found descriptions of mounds, caverns, gateways, sacred cows and the individual parts of a celestial barge. The most important element in these descriptions was the precise name of the thing. That was its magic.

The location of the Otherworld was in part the space through which the sun journeyed by day, across the heavens, but also at night when it passed unseen through an imagined dangerous realm to be ready to rise again in the eastern horizon. The Egyptians seem not to have visualized it literally and in relationship to the visible world, or at least to the land of Egypt, although certain aspects were geographically orientated. The West, for example, was the particular abode of the dead. However, the Book of the Dead was not encyclopaedic. Other 'books' developed particular aspects of the Otherworld in far more detail, whereas the Book of the Dead provided an overview.

What should modern readers make of the Book of the Dead? It helped to shape the mindset of many ancient Egyptians and so is an important source for understanding their thoughts. Outside mainstream or conventional Egyptology the Book of the Dead has proved of interest to people dissatisfied with a purely reductionist and scientific explanation for the nature of knowledge, who feel that whilst science explains how the universe works, knowledge of equal value, concerning the spiritual nature of man, lies within the self and that all religions contain a portion of an overarching truth.[4] The Egyptians, working with a very small set of labelled phenomena and limited tools of abstract philosophical debate, took a great delight in the richness of texture that their fascination with names and divine characteristics produced. Even though the details of their mythology are not those of a modern reader, the Egyptian view that all knowledge of the hidden workings of the universe as revealed by mythology has value and was to be accumulated respectfully is the antithesis of dogmatism. The view that the individual has his or her own personal universe – and actually *is* that universe – is, despite the strangeness of the Egyptian imagery, an oddly humanist stance.

1

BETWEEN TWO WORLDS

O you who cuts off heads and severs necks, who renders incoherent the spirits with respect to the magic which resides in them, you shall not see me with those eyes of yours out of which you see from [between] your knees. May you wander round with your face averted, may you catch sight of Shu's demons after you, to cut off your head and sever your neck – at the behest of the one who despoiled his Lord – on account of what you have said you would do to me: reduce me to incoherence, cut off my head, sever my neck, seal my mouth, on account of the magic that resides in me, just as you are wont to do to spirits with respect to the magic that resides in them. (Spell 90)

The Book of the Dead depended upon the power of words. Here the reader faces up to the possibility that a demon will deny him, by cutting off his head, even the use of the very magic spells that will guard against the dangers of the Otherworld. The Egyptians believed in and created a world of supernatural forces so vivid, powerful and inescapable, that controlling one's destiny within it was a central preoccupation. In life these forces manifested themselves through misfortune and illness, and after death the Egyptians faced the same forces in the Otherworld, for eternity. Both in this world and the next they existed alongside the named, conventional gods and goddesses who could be appealed to for assistance, although even they could not be relied upon and could even set out to pursue and harm an individual. Some of the spells of the Book of the Dead identify a reader's enemies: 'men, gods, spirits of the dead', according to Spell 148; 'men, gods, spirits, dead men, patricians, common people, sun-folk', according to Spell 42. Nowhere was safe.

Although the individual might fear the personal malevolence of these enemies they were part of a wider underlying threat to the order of the universe. Its principal manifestations were encountered by the sun-god on his voyages across the sky and through the dark regions of the night. Its most dramatic expression took the form of a giant serpent, Apep, whom the sun-god defeated with the help of friendly demons.

Fear of the often malignant powers of the supernatural led to a long tradition of protective texts composed and edited as defences. A properly equipped Egyptian household would possess collections of 'spells' for a variety of purposes written on rolls of papyrus, to counter malign spirits of the dead entering the house at night to steal the life of children, or to combat the pain and inflammation of scorpion stings, or to staunch anal haemorrhage. The spells were accompanied by instructions for making potions and magical objects over which the spells were spoken. These widely circulated spells give us today a picture of the Egyptian's imaginary world, with its set of gods, evil forces and symbols.

Papyrus in ancient Egypt was not expensive and was readily available. Many collections of 'spells' are likely to have been in circulation all the time, being bought, inherited, given as gifts, and carried from one town to another. They were part of the common currency of the literate part of the population (though this must have been fairly small, in the cities one might guess 10 per cent). Spells did not belong to a secret, deeply sacred category of writings: anyone who could write could make copies, create personal anthologies and, if one had the predisposition, compose new versions. The spells drew upon a fairly defined vocabulary and set of mythological concepts, making new versions relatively easy to compose, following the formulas. The same style of writing, drawing upon a more extended range of mythological elements, was employed to create the texts that prepared the spirit for what it would face after death. The Book of the Dead was a collection of these texts, the readers already familiar with its style and content from the texts used to protect the household.

The Book of the Dead first became popular during the New Kingdom. This was a time of great prosperity and stability during which Egypt maintained an imperial hold over the northern Sudan, Palestine and Syria. The country was run by a class of scribes (from whom the ranks of the priesthood were drawn). They wrote about themselves in self-confident terms, owned farmland and slaves, aspired to be the leading citizens of their community, sought to commemorate themselves for posterity with handsome (and expensive-to-build) tomb chapels, and gave themselves the chance of comfort after death through a well-appointed burial. These were the people for whom most of the copies of the Book of the Dead were made. There seems a contrast between the serenity of how they portrayed themselves – in their statues and in paintings in their tombs – and the fears and dangers expressed in the spells of household protection and of the Book of the Dead.

The Book of the Dead filled an ancient need. Many of its

spells appear in earlier versions written on the insides of wooden coffins, some of the earliest dating to around 2100 BC. The modern term for them is Coffin Texts. They appeared during a time of provincial rivalry in Egypt that led to civil war. Modern historians refer to this time as the First Intermediate Period, and it separated the age of pyramid building (the Old Kingdom) from a second period of stability and high cultural achievement (the Middle Kingdom). The subsequent history of Coffin Texts, and of the Book of the Dead which replaced them, seems, however, to owe little if anything to political uncertainty. The world of daily experience, of government and farming, was subject to unseen but sharply felt supernatural forces that a person's spirit would encounter even more closely after death regardless of who was in charge.

Kings – Egyptian Pharaohs – were not above the powers of these supernatural forces. Even before the Coffin Texts the burial chambers of the later pyramids (from that of King Unas onwards, *c.* 2345 BC) bore hieroglyphic texts (the Pyramid Texts) that set the king in the same ambivalent role of potential victim yet ultimate victor in the face of supernatural forces – a role that is developed in the Book of the Dead. In the New Kingdom the tombs of kings were no longer pyramids but underground galleries in the Valley of Kings at Thebes. Their walls were covered with pictures and texts which went far beyond the Book of the Dead in their creation of a hidden world of multiple dangers that faced both the sun-god and the king as he journeyed with the sun through the realm of the night.

For almost the first thousand years of its existence (starting from the early New Kingdom) the Book of the Dead was not standardized. That came later. The scribes who made a par-

ticular copy were conscious that there was a model to be followed, a text that they called the 'Coming Forth by Day'
(and we call the Book of the Dead). Mostly they followed an
existing copy, but its length and the order of its sections were
not binding. Richer people did not necessarily buy longer
versions. One of the short versions was owned by Yuya,
father-in-law of Amenhotep III, whose tomb was in the
Valley of Kings amongst the elite.[5] It seems that it took a long
time for a tradition to develop as to length and order, and only
settled from around 600 BC onwards, when a fairly set order of
192 Spells was followed.

Many of the spells are variations on a small number of
themes, and one could sometimes be substituted for another.
A scribe, having in front of him two similar but not identical
texts, might choose to copy them both. One episode of this
cut-and-paste approach became permanently incorporated
into the master versions, as recorded at the head of Spell 163:
'Spells taken from another papyrus as additions to the
"Coming Forth by Day".' More common, though, was a dili-
gent adherence to the master text, as expressed in an earnest
note added to a copy of the Book found in Yuya's tomb:
'Finished from its beginning to its end as found written,
having been set down, collated, checked, and corrected sign
by sign.'

The Book did not claim a single authorship, nor did
anyone put their name to a spell. Nor were the spells considered revelations of gods or spirits. The Book is anonymous
and generally avoids hints as to its place and time of composition. These were historical matters in which the Egyptians
took little interest. The authority that resided in these spells
mostly came simply from their content, sometimes reinforced
by an anonymous recommendation: 'It is a matter a million

times true; I have seen it and it has indeed come to pass through me' (Spell 19). A few of the spells, however, claimed the authority of great antiquity, or close association with a famous king. Thus Spell 30 was said to have been discovered at Hermopolis, a city famous as the centre of the cult of Thoth god of wisdom, in the reign of King Menkaura, builder of one of the three pyramids at Giza. He had lived around a thousand years before people began making copies of the Book of the Dead.

> This spell was found in Hermopolis, under the feet of this god. It was written on a block of mineral of Upper Egypt in the writing of the god himself, and was discovered in the time of the Majesty of the indicated king of Upper and Lower Egypt, Menkaura. It was the king's son Hordedef who found it while he was going around making an inspection of the temples.

Reinforcement of the spell's ancient authority came in the mention of its discoverer, Prince Hordedef. He was a son of King Khufu (builder of the Great Pyramid and grandfather of Menkaura), and was remembered by later generations as the author of a book of wise advice, the 'Teachings of Hordedef'.

Modern comments on the Book sometimes suggest that copies of it were acquired only for the funeral, to be buried with the corpse; that the person's spirit lived on after death and could read the copy then, and that the Book thus had no living readers. The Book's spells also primarily apply, in their general character and sometimes through direct statement, to situations faced by the spirit of a dead person. The findings of archaeology have not clarified whether the Book was read as literature. Papyrus generally does not survive well on the sites of ancient settlement, and so the absence of the Book of the

Dead from the reports of excavators who have dug into towns and cities is neither surprising nor significant.

Here and there, however, one will find statements that addressed the living readers of the Book's contents:

> If a man speaks this spell when he is in a state of purity, it means going forth after death into the day and assuming whatever shape he desires. As for anyone who shall read it daily for his own benefit, it means being hale on earth. He shall come forth from every fire and nothing evil shall reach him. (Spell 17)

> As for him who knows this spell, he will be a worthy spirit in the realm of the dead, and he will not die again in the realm of the dead, and he will eat in the presence of Osiris. As for him who knows it on earth, he will be like Thoth, he will be worshipped by the living, he will not fall to the power of the king or the hot rage of Bastet,* and he will proceed to a very happy old age. (Spell 135)

Here then is evidence that the Book of the Dead was read by the living. The image of the Egyptian 'who shall read it daily for his own benefit' suggests that Egyptians read it over a period of their lives. Did they discuss it with one another, seeking help with passages that were particularly difficult? The Book promised to place the reader at the centre of the universe. In doing this it might have made the Book the most widely read ancient Egyptian text. Through it a significant element in the population would then have gained access to the essence of ancient Egyptian thinking and culture. There are no comments in other written sources about people reading the Book, but that applies to Egyptian habits generally. Surviving written sources of all kinds from ancient Egypt are sparing in

---

*The 'hot rage of Bastet' (a feline goddess) could be a reference to infectious disease.

personal anecdotes or in mentions of what people did in their lives. Our understanding of Egyptian character and how they engaged with their religious system still rests on very inadequate evidence.

There is an extensive treatment of personal moral conduct contained within Spell 125 (discussed in detail in Chapter 5). If people made themselves familiar with the Book, especially as they grew older, that part of the text would act as moral instruction, alongside the more secular books of guidance to life, the 'teachings' of famous wise men, that were a popular form of literature. Seeing the Book of the Dead in a positive light, as a source of instruction, with moral values, is a view that Egyptologists have been reluctant to accept.

By the time of the New Kingdom the core text of the spells was very ancient and some was hard to understand. In Spell 17, a scribe has decided, instead of simply copying an old text, to explain and enrich the imagery. The original text described in what ways god is great. The scribe divided the passage into sections and, after each one (using red ink for his editorial voice, which subsequently became part of the master text and was copied over the centuries), inserted his own expansions of meaning. In the following translation (a small sample of a longer text) the original red-ink passages are in italics.

'I am the Great God, the self-created.' *Who is he?* The Great God, the self-created, is water, he is Nun, father of the gods. *Otherwise said:* He is Ra.

'He who created his names, Lord of the Ennead.' *Who is he?* It is Ra who created his names and his members, it means the coming into existence of those gods who are in his suite.

'I am he who is not opposed among the gods.' *Who is he?* He is Atum who is in his sun-disc. *Otherwise said:* He is Ra when he rises in the eastern horizon of the sky.

'To me belongs yesterday, I know tomorrow.' *What does it mean?* As for yesterday, that is Osiris. As for tomorrow, that is Ra on that day in which the foes of the Lord of All were destroyed and his son Horus was made to rule. *Otherwise said:* That is the day of the 'We-remain' festival, when the burial of Osiris was ordered by his father Ra.

'I am that great phoenix which is in Heliopolis, the supervisor of what exists.' *Who is he?* He is Osiris. As for what exists, that means his injury. *Otherwise said:* That means his corpse. *Otherwise said:* It means eternity and everlasting. As for eternity, it means daytime; as for everlasting, it means night. (Spell 17)

The original text made a series of declarations concerning the multiple characteristics of God. The scribe supplies more explicit identifications after posing simple questions. In all but one of the declarations, however, a second opinion is given after a second question. We cannot tell if these are all ideas that came into the mind of the unknown scribe who wrote what became the standard version of Spell 17, or if he consulted another's commentary and wanted to include its contents.

The identifications are with a set of prime movers in the universe: Atum the creator, Ra the sun, Osiris the king of the realm of the dead, and Nun, the watery element which preceded the separation of the forms of things. He also refers to them as if they are names for a single ultimate divinity who is simultaneously one of this set of four. In connecting these figures together, the scribe has performed a particularly impressive piece of reduction of religious tradition. Two of the foundation myths of ancient Egypt, which are constantly referred to in the Book of the Dead, are of quite independent origin.

One myth concerns the violent death and coming again to life of Osiris, a mythical king who became ruler of the dead and the representative of righteousness and of the stability of society. The other portrays the sun as the source of all life, whose daily course across the heavens was seen as a triumph over the forces of disturbance that he faced during the nightly passage through the Otherworld. In the Book of the Dead the two gods and their imagery keep their original characters, yet simultaneously merge. The scribe's comments on Spell 17 set up suggestive pairings. The sun–god Ra is declared to be tomorrow, eternity and daytime; Osiris is declared to be yesterday, everlasting and night. And yet the two are bridged. 'Tomorrow' is when Ra destroys foes who are clearly those of Osiris, the result of which is that the son of Osiris, Horus, can take over the rule of the living. This is not looking ahead to a single apocalyptic moment, however. Tomorrow is portrayed as an ever-present occasion when this event is about to happen. As a way of succinctly pointing to Ra as the initiator of these actions and Osiris as the beneficiary, Osiris becomes the 'son' of Ra.

Spell 17 illustrates the Egyptians' fondness for elegant variation, in a style of writing that constantly resonated with their stock of myths. The piling up of allusions is saying something quite simple: god is great (and male), and he is the master of creation, of continuing life, and of the eternity of time.

The god in Spell 17 is praised as 'Ra who created his names and his members'. The concept of names fascinated the Egyptians, and with reason. If names bestowed identity, what remained independent of the name? If the great god called himself Ra, then Atum, and then Osiris, in what way was he not all of these gods? Or in what ways did these gods have a separate existence other than when called upon by their names? It is an important philosophical point. Even though they did not reflect on it in the abstract, the Egyptians seem well aware that imaginary beings need to have a name to exist at all, and that this was something that the individual therefore had control over. By extension, it opened the way for the reader to take possession of the identity of such beings, by the simple step of claiming their names.

The same applied to all beings that existed in the Otherworld. If you knew their names, it made you feel that in some way they were subservient to you. Names provided a channel of control. The Book constantly tells the reader the names of things in the Otherworld for this reason, to bestow power. So Spell 148 proclaims: 'Hail to you, you who shine in your disc, a living soul who goes up from the horizon! I know you and I know your name. I know the names of the seven cows and their bull who give bread and beer, who are beneficial to souls and who provide daily portions.' Then follows their names: 'The much beloved, red of hair', for example, and 'Storm in the sky which wafts the god aloft'. After having done this, the text continues, with no word of explanation as if it is the most logical thing to do, to provide 'The names of the four steering-oars of the sky', building on the automatic image in the Egyptian mind of the ornate boat that conveyed the sun across the sky. Navigating the Otherworld became, in effect, a scholarly task. Instead of bravery and fortitude it was knowing the technical terms that got you through what faced you in the Otherworld: perpetual encounters with its places and beings that did not quite amount to a journey.

Did the Egyptians find it profitable to read passages from the Book of the Dead and learn by heart, even recite as a mantra, the names of the seven cows and their bull, for example? We simply do not know. Fear pervades the Book. It seems perverse to think that the Egyptians would not have sought to calm their fears by reading about them over and over again. The opportunity to learn the names of the dangerous entities revealed in the Book of the Dead – and thus conquer their fears – might have drawn them irresistibly to master its contents through regular study. Humans in all civilizations create fearful worlds of the imagination. Through religions and philosophies we then try to come to terms and cope with them. The way to cope with the Otherworld, by learning names and short passages of text, looks to have been a rational and very satisfying measure to take.

2

WORKING WITH MYTHS

'O Thoth, what is it that has come about through the Children of Nut? They have made war, they have raised up tumult, they have done wrong, they have created rebellion, they have done slaughter, they have created imprisonment, they have reduced what was great to what is little in all that we have made; show greatness, O Thoth!' So says Atum . . .

READER: 'O Atum, how comes it that I travel to a desert which has no water and no air, and which is deep, dark and unsearchable?'

ATUM: 'Live in it in content.'

READER: 'But there is no love-making there.'

ATUM: 'I have given spirit-being instead of water, air and love-making; contentment in place of bread and beer'; so says Atum. 'Do not be sorry for yourself, for I will not suffer you to lack.'

READER: 'But every god has taken his place in the Barque of Millions of Years.'

ATUM: 'Your seat now belongs to your son Horus (so says Atum) and *he* will despatch the Elders, he will rule from your seat, he will inherit the throne which is in the Island of Fire.'

READER: 'Command that I may see his equal, for my face will see the face of the Lord of All. What will be the duration of my life?' So said he.

ATUM: 'You shall be for millions on millions of years, a lifetime of millions of years. I will despatch the Elders and destroy all that I have made; the earth shall return to the Abyss, to the surging flood, as in its original state. But I will remain with Osiris. I will transform myself into something else, namely a serpent, without men knowing or the gods seeing. How good is what I have done for Osiris, even more than for all the gods. I have given him the desert, and his son Horus is the heir on his throne which is in the Island of Fire. I have made what appertains to his place in the Barque of Millions of Years, and Horus is firm on his throne in order to found his establishments.'

READER: 'But the soul of Seth will travel further than all the gods.'

ATUM: 'I have caused his soul which is in the barque to be restrained so that the body of the god may be afraid.'

READER: 'O my father Osiris, do for me what your father Ra did for you, so that I may be long-lived on earth, that my throne may be well-founded, that my heir may be in good health, that my tomb may be long-enduring, and that these servants of mine may be on earth; let my enemies be split open, may the Scorpion be on their bones, for I am your son, O my father Ra; do this for me for the sake of my life, welfare and health, for Horus is firmly established on his throne, and let my lifetime come to attain to the blessed state.' (Spell 175)

Spell 175 is a dialogue between the creator god Atum and the reader (who in this spell identifies himself with the god Osiris), in which the god Thoth, who represents wisdom, acts rather like an intelligent bystander. It has the heading 'Spell for not dying again'. This is not a reference to reincarnation but points to the ancient Egyptian fear that the spirit of the deceased, having successfully established an existence in the Otherworld, might suffer final annihilation. The spell's power lay in recalling certain elements of Egyptian myths that, in a general way, stood for the triumph of the righteous life over forces of upheaval. These citations of mythical events were powerful instruments to be wielded and were, in a way, as much part of the magic as explicit commands and directions.

The Book of the Dead constantly alludes to three myths that make up the basis of Egyptian religious belief. They are sufficiently different to suggest that they had separate origins,

although the Book weaves them together and implicitly uni-
fies them. Each myth was built around one of three
foundation deities, Osiris, Atum and Ra. They did not com-
pete or struggle, for their realms of interest were different.
One, the myth of Osiris, provided historical authority for a
belief in personal continuity both in the sense of legitimate
inheritance from father to son and, beyond death, in an afterlife. The second myth was an account of how the material
universe was created from nothingness by an ulterior creating
force, visualized as the god Atum whose name meant 'completion'. The third myth described the source of the world's
energy or life force, in the figure of the sun-god Ra.

The myth of Osiris, or the strands of myth that gathered
around him, are mostly preserved as short allusions. The
Egyptians were far less interested in what the gods did than
what the gods stood for. The Book of the Dead, like other
similar texts, includes very brief episodes in which gods inter-
act, but no myth narratives of any length. For full versions of
the Osiris myth we have to wait until near the end of ancient
Egyptian civilization, when Greek and Roman authors
encountered Egypt as travellers or residents. The most detailed
account is written by an ancient Greek scholar-priest,
Plutarch, around AD 100.[6]

The Osiris myth is centred on a confrontation between
gods. On the one side is a family group: Osiris, a lawful king
of Egypt in an undefined time, his wife (and sister) Isis, and
their son, Horus. Their opponent is Seth (sometimes the
brother of Osiris, sometimes of Horus) who, with a naturally
violent and rebellious disposition, and sometimes accompanied by a gang of followers, murders Osiris and dismembers
his body. Isis protects her son Horus who avenges his father
through victory over Seth and becomes the next king of

Egypt. Because of Horus's loyalty, Osiris regains life as king of the realm of the dead, his body whole again.

The details vary from one source to another; the myth was not so much a story as a grouping of characters who illustrated more than one spiritual and ethical theme. One lesson was that a stable society rested on family continuity and especially upon the transfer of male authority from one generation to the next, aided by the protecting mother. It provided the model for the royal succession and for family life generally. The Osiris myth also demonstrated life after death: an eternal spiritual existence was on offer to every person. The only condition for afterlife was that the spirit of the dead person be judged as having passed a life free of misbehaviour. There was no test of faith or community of believers. Faith was simply taken for granted.

Osiris was described as a king. 'Hail to you who made the gods, the vindicated king of Upper and Lower Egypt, Osiris, who founded the Two Lands with his potent deeds' (Spell 15). The tomb of one of Egypt's earliest kings, located in the desert behind the ancient town of Abydos in Upper Egypt, came to be known as the tomb of Osiris. It gave focus to Osiris worship and became a place of pilgrimage. This ancient 'discovery' of the tomb of Osiris at Abydos fixed him in historic time as one of Egypt's ancestral kings from the earliest period of history. Whilst it remains impossible to trace how ancient the myth was, we know that his popular cult only developed many centuries after the beginnings of ancient Egyptian history, to be more precise, between the end of the Old Kingdom and the beginning of the Middle (c. 2050 BC). At this time, people began to invoke his name on tombstones in their local cemeteries and, having undertaken a voyage of pilgrimage to the holy site of Abydos, left memorial tablets so that their names would be not far from the presence of Osiris.

In many places in the Book of the Dead the owner of the text is addressed by his or her name that the scribe has inserted. In some cases the name is prefixed by the name Osiris so that the man or woman becomes 'Osiris so-and-so' and therefore *is* Osiris. The papyrus that belonged to the scribe Any begins a hymn of praise to the sun god (Spell 15) with the words: 'Worship of Ra when he rises on the horizon until the occurrence of his setting in life. Word spoken by Osiris, the scribe Any: "Hail to you Ra, at your rising".' Yet even so, Egyptians faced judgement of their earthly deeds after death by a tribunal headed by the real Osiris, who remained a separate figure, as 'ruler of eternity'. To ward off a negative judgement, Egyptians would declare themselves 'true of voice'; hence predicting a successful outcome to their judgement.

The Osiris myth was not simply a myth about the afterlife, but also a story about Horus, Osiris's son. Many texts refer to a long-running contest between Horus and Seth, who appear as a pair of youths competing against one another – for personal victory, but also for symbolic supremacy in a struggle between harmony and discord. Horus was the ideal son, the ideal heir to the throne of Egypt: an embodiment of every living king who ascended the throne of Egypt. Every king took a special name denoting his particular identity as an incarnation of Horus. In contrast, the unruly Seth was associated with otherness, with the deserts, with foreignness, with stormy weather, as well as with violence and turbulence amongst people.

Sometimes Egyptian texts refer to violent mutilation that occurred during the duel. Seth attacked the eye of Horus, who is often portrayed as a falcon. The restoration of the eye of Horus was a symbol of wholeness and completion. Horus in turn castrates Seth. At other times the quarrel is simply a squabble between brothers, who play practical jokes. The quarrel disturbs the company of nine great gods – the Ennead – presided over by Geb, representative of earth. They form a tribunal and pronounce judgement against Seth, who accepts his defeat. This final act was itself a powerful symbol to the Egyptians of the supremacy of law and of the exercise of judgement through respected groups of senior figures. The unruly elements of the universe were to be tamed by patrician judgement and not by physical coercion. And Seth benefited. His willingness to accept the verdict against him illuminated his benign qualities. Until very late in Egyptian history, Seth was not fully the embodiment of evil. He could also stand side by side with Horus, each of them a symbol of one half of the kingdom of Egypt, Horus for the north (Lower Egypt) and Seth for the south (Upper Egypt). When paired in this way Seth lost his foreign and unruly aspect and became simply the patron god of Upper Egypt, a status derived from a time in late prehistory when the city in Upper Egypt most associated with him (now an archaeological site known as Nagada) was a regional capital.

The god Atum also regularly appears in the Book of the Dead. In Egyptian myth he was a creator by whose agency an inert primordial substance – watery but formless – was transformed into four eternal conditions each one of which was given a name that is virtually beyond modern translation. 'Infinity, nothingness, nowhere and darkness' is one set of possibilities. Each of these possessed a male and female version, so creating a set of eight, from which foundation gods emerged (amongst them Osiris, Isis and Seth). Thus the universe began to take shape. Embodied within Atum was the god Shu, of light and air, creating the environment humans needed for their survival.

The third myth constantly alluded to in the Book of the Dead concerned the sun-god Ra. The rising of the sun brought light, warmth and life and was, from early times, central to the thinking of the Egyptians. His symbol was a pointed stone, given architectural expression in the pyramid-tombs of the earlier kings and in the tall obelisks that sometimes were placed in front of the larger temples in the New Kingdom. Every king of Egypt was a 'son of Ra'. The Egyptians pictured the sun-god making a cyclic daily journey in an ornate boat or barque which conveyed him across the sky between sunrise and sunset and returned him at night ready to start again the following morning. The nightly journey took him through the Otherworld. He navigated a course through a series of guarded gateways and faced up to attacks by hostile beings that represented the forces of disturbance in the universe, often visualized as a giant serpent, named Apep. Sometimes they were marshalled by the god Seth and his 'gang'.

The gods had identities rather than characters or personalities. In some cases they were also concepts or symbols of types of power. They could be grouped in hierarchies, using the standard family grouping of father/mother/offspring to supply the model and the terminology of their interrelationships of authority: thus the family group of Osiris, Isis and Horus, with Seth the black sheep. Gods were also linked by merging their names. The best known example is Amun-Ra. In this compound the name of Amun, the god of the city of Thebes, the home of the ruling house of Egypt for many centuries, was joined to that of the sun-god Ra. Amun, even without the added name Ra, became in many respects the sun-god himself. In the Book of the Dead, it might be noted, the names Amun and Amun-Ra are rare (Amun occurs in Spell 171 near the end of a list of gods) and many people's copies contained no spell mentioning him. The sun-god is always simply Ra. This reflects the way that the god Amun rose to prominence following the success of the city of Thebes in the civil war of the First Intermediate Period. By this time the theological tradition out of which the Book of the Dead later grew was already established by the Pyramid Texts and Coffin Texts. Amun evidently did not readily fit in. Moreover, uncertainty developed in some Egyptian minds about the propriety of depicting Ra in the fully human shape that was the standard image of Amun. The reign of King Akhenaten during the New Kingdom (1352–1336 BC) witnessed an attempt to purge the cult of the sun by destroying all images of and references to Amun and by emphasizing the disc of the sun as its only proper image. Although this intolerance was at variance with the way that Egyptians normally handled religious matters and Akhenaten was later vilified, the rarity of Amun's name in subsequent copies of the Book of the Dead does imply a reservation about his position in theology.

In the Book of the Dead the names and identities of Ra and Osiris are intertwined and made complementary, but the Egyptians never created a compound deity called Osiris-Ra. Subtle rules of appropriateness evidently ruled this out. Instead language was used that merged them yet kept them separate, as in Spell 182: Speech of Thoth: 'I cause Ra to go to rest as Osiris, Osiris having gone to rest at the going to rest of Ra . . .' Spell 181 takes this further. The reader addresses Osiris and compares him to Ra. 'His sun-disc is your sun-disc; his rays are your rays . . . You have seated yourself on your pure throne which Geb, who loves you, made for you; you receive him in your arms in the West, you cross the sky daily, you convey him to his mother Nut when he goes to rest daily in the West in the Barque of Ra, together with Horus who loves you.' Osiris, along with his son Horus, now makes the daily crossing of the sky (personified as the goddess Nut), setting in the west, and so is imagined as another form of the sun-god. In ancient Egypt the gods were often parallel concepts able, not exactly to change places with one another, but to blend and to harmonize. It was not always a two-way process, however. The harmonization was dependent on the supremacy of the sun-god. Osiris might be a manifestation of Ra, but not the other way round.

In Spell 175, the 'Spell for not dying again', several myths are intertwined. The spell builds up to a recapitulation of the triumph of Osiris over the hostility of Seth, a parallel to what the reader hopes will be his own triumph over the forces of decay. The myth that is summarized, however, is not the original version. It has become entwined with that of the sun-god, now senior to Osiris. The sun-god appears in two forms, mostly as Atum but at the end as Ra. Seth, too, is transformed into a celestial god, journeying in the sun's barque. This provides the opportunity to introduce an alternative myth of hostility, one that belongs to the world of the sun-god. Instead of a murderous Seth, hostility is manifested in the incurable rebelliousness that humanity – the 'Children of Nut', the goddess of the sky – shows towards its creator, Atum. Atum's response to the rebellion is to destroy the world, returning it to its formless pre-elemental state. There is no sign that the Egyptians saw this as a threat of future real time. It was not an apocalyptic vision. Like all Egyptian myths it is a metaphor outside the space and time of the world of humans. The reader glimpses with horror the formless chaos that is the result, devoid of water, air and sexual reproduction. Atum's reassurance is that the reader becomes Osiris through the simple expedient of being addressed as such. The reader now has Horus as his son, who will ensure the continuity of family authority.

At the end the reader, having for a moment identified with Osiris, now addresses him as a separate person. The final fear is revealed: the reader's tomb might suffer through disruption to the continuity of family inheritance. The second dying, it seems, could come about through the breaking of the links that bind together the earthly family and its spiritual counterpart. It is only these final passages that address directly the stated intention of the spell. What function does the rest of it perform? It must be that the recounting of the myths themselves are the magic words. The abundant references to gods are the words of power. The myths serve only as respectful introductions to them. The scene-shifting narrative that links them was not important in itself.

3

THE LANDSCAPE OF THE OTHERWORLD

I arrive at the Island of the Horizon-Dwellers, I go out from the holy gate. *What is it?* It is the Field of Rushes, which produced the provisions for the gods who are round about the shrine. As for that holy gate, it is the gate of the Supports of Shu. *Otherwise said:* It is the gate of the Otherworld. *Otherwise said:* It is the door through which my father Atum passed when he proceeded to the eastern horizon of the sky. (Spell 17)

As for that mountain of Bakhu on which the sky rests, it is in the east of the sky. It is three hundred rods long and one hundred and fifty rods broad. Sebek, Lord of Bakhu, is in the east of that mountain. His temple is of carnelian. A serpent is on top of that mountain. It is thirty cubits long, eight cubits of its forepart are of flint, and its teeth gleam. I know the name of this serpent which is on the mountain. Its name is 'He who is in his burning'. Now after a while he will turn his eyes against Ra, and a stoppage will occur in the Sacred Barque and a great vision among the crew, for he will swallow up seven cubits of the great waters. Seth will project a lance of iron against him and will make him vomit up all that he has swallowed. Seth will place him before him and will say to him with magic power: 'Get back at the sharp knife which is in my hand! I stand before you, navigating aright and seeing afar.' (Spell 108)

If you lived on as a spirit after death, where would you be? The Egyptians saw two possibilities, one local and situated in the real world, and the other located in the realm of the imagination. These two locations coexisted. In the first the spirits of the dead remained close to the tomb, if not within it, although they could also venture out at night and do harm in the houses of the living, especially to young children. The second location for the dead was the *Duat*, the Otherworld, a dangerous and complex world through which the spirits navigated.

The geography of the Otherworld was imagined in rich detail. The Egyptians filled it with invented topographic features, places then referred to in mythological allusions. It possessed mountains, fields, waterways, gates, and sinister 'caverns' and 'mounds'. The landscape was sometimes made of unusual and precious materials: a temple of carnelian, two trees of turquoise, walls of iron around the Field of Rushes. They were larger than normal, though not impossibly so: the serpent on the mountains was 30 cubits long (around 15 metres), the barley that grew in the Field of Rushes was 5 cubits tall (2.5 metres). For a people capable of raising statues 18 metres high (36 cubits) and giant pieces of architecture, including the pyramids, that long predate the Book of the Dead, the scale of the Otherworld is quite modest.

The Otherworld was a defined and limited place. The sun god voyaged through it nightly. The entrance to the Otherworld is described in Spell 17 as an 'Island of the Horizon-Dwellers' where the 'gate of the Otherworld' is located. This leads to the place of sunrise, 'the eastern horizon of the sky', by a way already taken by the creator god Atum. The Egyptians loved to pack in extra weighty allusions. The holy gate was also the location of the four supports of Shu, the personification of the atmosphere and of the brightness of the light that it conveyed. The spatial logic is lost: the four supports should have been as widely separated as the size of the universe, but the grandeur of the idea here takes precedence over logic.

The Otherworld accommodated the kingdom of Osiris, where the dead would be judged and where, assuming that they were declared innocent of wrongdoing, they would dwell forever. The spirit of the dead Egyptian approached Osiris via a series of numbered gateways. Each gateway had a guardian who only allowed passage through when addressed by name. Spell 144 tells us that seven gates guard the presence of Osiris. Each of the seven gates has a keeper, a guard, and an announcer. '"He whose face is inverted, the many-shaped" is the name of the keeper of the first gate; "Eavesdropper" is the name of him who guards it; "The loud-voiced" is the name of the announcer.' In Spell 146, however, the 'mysterious portals of the House of Osiris in the Field of Rushes' number twenty-one. Each one has its guardian, who this time is female, though provided with a male door-keeper. The eighth guardian is 'Hot of flames, destructive of heat, sharp of blade, swift of hand, who kills without warning, whom none pass by for fear of her pain'. Here perhaps is an echo of the protocol of the living kings. Access to the king in his palace was regulated, and to reach the king a visitor would pass along passageways, halls and through many doorways until, after much questioning and inspection by palace guards and officials, the throne room was reached.

Although the Egyptians believed that the Otherworld occupied a real space, there was no overall map of the Otherworld in the Book of the Dead. No route is described from, say, 'that mountain of Bakhu' to the Field of Rushes, and the kingdom of Osiris was not signposted from either. Around 2000 BC (early Middle Kingdom), the Coffin Texts included a map of winding waterways to illustrate a journey that the dead would take, but the map covers only one set of mythological points.[7] It does not chart localities mentioned in other parts of the Coffin Texts. To what extent the Egyptians mapped their own real surroundings is hard to tell. Only one map has been discovered from ancient Egypt, on a piece of papyrus found somewhere in western Thebes. It shows a mountainous zone where gold was to be found, and has been identified as part of the Wadi Hammamat in the Red Sea hills.[8] A school exercise used to train scribes contains a test of Palestinian geographical knowledge that a scribe might find useful if he were accompanying the Egyptian army.[9] But this was entirely verbal. By and large the ancient Egyptians had a pre-cartographic mindset.

Other than in the Book of the Dead and related religious compositions, landscape real or imagined was not a theme of great interest in Egyptian literature or art. A few tales from ancient Egypt have survived, written on papyrus, set in fantasy places. In one a sailor is shipwrecked on a magic island inhabited by a giant serpent. The snake is lonely and in need of human company. In another a prince travels to a distant country and rescues an imprisoned princess. These stories are similar to fairy tales of today and so did not carry the weight of religious myth of the Book of the Dead. The places themselves are barely described. Even in a popular retelling of the quarrelling gods Horus and Seth, found in a papyrus that had been part of a private library in an ancient Egyptian village, and in which they appear as young men who constantly fight, the landscape through which they move is barely sketched in. A few localities, such as a hall named 'Field of Rushes', cross-reference the Book of the Dead but they are no more than names.

The walls of tombs and temples often depicted the life of the fields or the joys of the desert hunt. The centre of interest was always the people and the animals. The landscape was reduced to a few stock images that created the right setting. A rare exception is a scene in the temple of Queen Hatshepsut at Deir el-Bahari, western Thebes, that dates to the early New Kingdom (1473–1458 BC). It records an expedition to the land of Punt, probably an area in modern Eritrea. The artists have included details of an African village landscape, although again as background to the main theme, which showed the trading of African incense for Egyptian manufactured goods.

Modern Egypt takes in a huge expanse of sand and gravel desert, of wadis and rocky table lands. It has an extensive coastline, along the Mediterranean and Red Seas. To the ancient Egyptians, however, these lay beyond the natural confines of Egypt. The desert, which housed many of the cemeteries of the dead, was associated with death and danger. In Spell 175, quoted in the last chapter, the desert is described as a sort of hell. The reader complains: 'O Atum, how does it happen that I travel to a desert which has no water and no air, and which is deep, dark and unsearchable?' When Atum replies 'Live there in contentment', the deceased laments: 'But there is no love-making there!'

Egypt was, to the ancient Egyptians, the Nile Valley north of Aswan. The Nile ran down a cleft in the surrounding desert plateau carpeted with rich dark silt, until eventually, just north of the location of modern Cairo, it divided into several channels and meandered across the flat muddy landscape of the Nile delta. The descriptions of the Otherworld were extensions of this familiar landscape rather than the desert we tend to associate with modern Egypt.

> I know those two trees of turquoise between which Ra goes forth, which have grown up at the Supports of Shu at that gate of the Lord of the East from which Ra goes forth. I know that Field of Rushes which belongs to Ra, the walls of which are of iron. The height of the barley is five cubits, its ear is two cubits, and its stalk three cubits; its emmer wheat is seven cubits, its ear is of three cubits and its stalk of four cubits. They are spirits, each nine cubits tall, who reap it in the presence of the Souls of the Easterners. (Spell 109)

The Field of Rushes, which is sometimes also called the Field of Offerings, is an exaggerated version of the cultivated fields of the floodplain at harvest time. Spell 110 describes the extensive scope of the fields, in which take place 'ploughing therein, reaping and eating therein, drinking therein, copulating, and doing everything that was once done on earth by the reader'.

Few Egyptians would have been able to recall from memory the sharply pointed peaks of Sinai or of the Red Sea hills. These were distant places reached only by expeditions sent out in search of minerals or trade goods. To most Egyptians, mountains meant the tawny cliffs that hem the Nile Valley south of Cairo and Memphis and which, in some localities, break into separate pointed masses. They might have thought of the western cliffs behind the cemetery and the mortuary temples of Thebes for the Mountain of Bakhu of Spell 108, which similarly had a temple on its eastern side.

The 'Mountain of Bakhu' was a dangerous haunt for the newly dead Egyptian. It was visualized as on the edge of their valley world, beyond which lay the hostile realm of the desert. On the mountain, during the nightly voyage of Ra, the giant serpent threatened the sun-god. Spell 108 briefly describes a drama in which Seth reveals the hidden benign side to his character. His natural fierceness can, on occasions, be harnessed for good. Seth threatened the serpent to protect Ra with a weapon of iron, a little-used material in Egypt and like Seth alien in character.

The most distinctive features of the landscape of the Otherworld are the caverns and the mounds. Mounds on the Nile floodplain had more than one origin. Some were natural deposits of sand, gravel and soft rock that broke through the floodplain and provided a dry place on which a settlement could grow, such as the ancient city of Edfu south of modern Luxor. Most natural mounds lay in the delta in the north. Other mounds were places of abandoned settlement, where collapsed mud-brick walls gradually returned to the soil, and tall coarse grass grew. The city of Thebes stood upon a mound which the Egyptians called 'the high place at the earth's beginning' suggesting – correctly by the time of the New Kingdom – a site that was very ancient.

'Caverns' (or we could translate the word as 'voids') are harder to place in the landscape of ancient Egypt. The word generally signified holes and cavities of various types but in the Book of the Dead it remains unclear what the concept evoked in the Egyptian mind.

The book of worshipping the gods of the caverns. What a man should say there when he reaches them in order to go in to see this god in the Great Mansion of the Otherworld. 'Hail to you, gods of the caverns which are in the West! Hail to you, door-keepers of the Otherworld who guard this god, and who bring news to the presence of Osiris! . . . May you guide the reader, may you open the portals for him, may the earth open its caverns to him, may you make him triumphant over his enemies.' (Spell 127)

Caverns were places where gods dwelt, though not the familiar gods that were cited by name. A separate and more specialized composition, a mixture of text and pictures carved on the walls of some of the tombs in the Valley of Kings (and given the modern name Book of Caverns), depicts rows of them, each one containing an unnamed god or goddess sometimes accompanied by a serpent.

> The fifth mound – green. The reader says: 'As for this Mound of Spirits by which men do not pass, the spirits who are in it are seven cubits from their buttocks, and they live on the shades of the inert ones. As for the Mound of Spirits, open your roads for me until I pass you by when I travel to the beautiful West.' (Spell 149)

The caverns and the mounds of the Book of the Dead have characteristics of their own: shapes and colours and distinctive occupants. Some of them were depicted in accompanying illustrations. Spell 149 describes fourteen mounds, eleven of them 'green', three of them 'yellow'. The pictures, however, deviate from the shape of the mound depicted in the hieroglyphic sign that was used to write the word, a low curving rise on which grows stylized vegetation. 'Mound' is evidently being used as a synonym for sacred place. In Spell 149 each mound has a different shape. Some of them are hollow and chamber-like. One turns out to be identical with the Field of Rushes. The sixth mound is a 'cavern sacred to the gods, secret from spirits and inaccessible to the dead'. Others are mountains or towns. The fourteenth diverts the Nile and 'causes it to come laden with barley. The snake that belongs to it is in the caverns of Elephantine at the source of the Nile.' In Spell 127 the caverns are the same as the gateways that guard the place of Osiris.

All of these various topographic features are places of

unearthly power, potential obstacles with whose denizens the reader must negotiate to maintain progress. The journey through the Otherworld with all its obstacles is one of the dominant themes of the Book of the Dead. What, though, is the ultimate destination? The answer seems to be, none. Eternity is motion, a dream-like passage from one checkpoint to the next. Spirits make visits; one of them is to the presence of Osiris, another is to the Field of Rushes and its super-abundant harvests. But these are end-points that exist in parallel to one another.

In the spirit's wandering through the Otherworld, it is hard to recognize a spiritual quest. The reader does not expect to ascend to higher planes of knowledge either of the self or the outside world. The blissful peace that comes from separation from the material world and closer proximity to god is not a concept that the ancient Egyptians developed. Instead, the experience of life after death was a continuous dangerous struggle and the Book of the Dead protects spirits of the dead from these dangers. By reading and learning the names and characteristics of the Otherworld and its parts, Egyptians could ward off the evils. Having invented a world of fears, the Egyptians set about creating practical ways to overcome them.

The topographic details of the Otherworld – like the gods themselves – shift identity. They are hard to tie down. They stand in for each other, so that mounds, caverns and gates can refer to sacred localities in Egypt, despite these localities not necessarily having the shape of, say, a mound. The Egyptians were unperturbed by a constant tacit admission that the varied images of belief were ways of perceiving a few basic truths: the singularity of god, the survival of the spirit, and that the Otherworld was a turbulent state from which there was no escape and into which death would cast you for eternity. The fearful world of the Book of the Dead suggests the Egyptians had an uneasy state of mind but it was not the way they felt all the time. Secular sources show that, in other moods, Egyptians could view the world more confidently.

The ancient Egyptians were a people untouched by the monotheistic religious concepts that subsequently came to dominate a large part of the world and have given modern society the view that religion, whatever the differences in the details, has a certain form, dogmatically maintained: a canonical text divinely revealed to select humans that can be explained but not modified, a demand for loyalty of belief (and thus separation from unbelievers) even when this belief, held by sects, is a variant interpretation of a common sacred text. The Egyptian spiritual experience – and in particular the relationship between language and concept – was different. In its lack of certainties and absence of dogmatism the Egyptian view is almost an early form of relativism.

VOYAGES AND PATHWAYS

Behold the starry sky is in Heliopolis, and the sun-folk are in Kheraha. The god is born, his fillet is bound on, his oar is grasped, and the reader gives judgement with them in the lotus-barque at the dockyard of the gods. The reader takes over the barque in it which has lotus-flowers on its ends. The reader ascends to the sky. The reader sails in it to Nut, he sails in it with Ra, he sails in it with apes, he repels the waves which are over yonder polar region of Nut at that stairway of Sebeg. (Spell 136A)

Spell for bringing a ferry-boat in the realm of the dead
'O ferryman, bring me this which was brought to Horus on account of his eye, and which was brought to Seth on account of his testicles. There leaps up the Eye of Horus which fell in the eastern side of the sky so that it may protect itself from Seth. O Mahaf, as you are provided with life, awaken Aqen for me, for see, I have come.'
   'Who are you that comes?'
   'I am the beloved of my father . . .'
   'Do you say that you would cross to the eastern side of the sky? If you cross what will you do?'
   'I will raise up his head . . .'
   'O Mahaf, as you are endowed with life, awaken Aqen for me, for see, I have come.'
   'Why should I awaken Aqen for you?'

'That he may bring me the built-up boat of Khnum from the Lake
of Feet.'

'But she is in pieces and stored in the dockyard.'

'Take her larboard side and fix it to the stern; take her starboard
side and fix it to the bow.'

*'But she has no planks, she has no end-pieces, she has no
rubbing-pieces, she has no oar-loops.'*

'Her planks are the drops of moisture which are on the lips of
Babai . . .'

'Tell me my name,' say the oars.

'The fingers of Horus the Elder' are your names.

'Tell me my name,' says the bailer.

'The hand of Isis which swabs up the blood from the Eye of Horus'
is your name. (Spell 99)

The Otherworld was a place of journeys, with multiple des-
tinations and obstacles to negotiate. One particularly
important journey for the spirit of the dead Egyptian was to
join, or to command, the celestial boat in which the sun–god
Ra made his nightly voyages. In Spell 136A the journey
begins in the 'dockyard of the gods' in Heliopolis, the centre
for the cult of Ra, especially in his early–morning manifestation. The sun–god's reappearance at dawn was his rebirth and
his resumption of authority, symbolized in Egyptian mythology by the tying on of his 'fillet', a headband that signified the
male coming of age. Ra sailed with apes who were thought to
greet the sun at dawn. A frieze of apes is carved along the top
of the façade of the temple of Rameses II at Abu Simbel in
Nubia, and around the base of the obelisk of the same king in
front of Luxor temple, the obelisk itself a point of commun-
ion with the sun. In an assertion of personal empowerment,
characteristic of the Book of the Dead, in Spell 99 the reader
takes command of the boat with no hint that he has violated
the dignity of the sun–god. At the same time, he joins the tri-

bunal of gods who judge the dispute between Horus and Seth.

Boats were advanced technology for the ancient Egyptians.[10] They were the most complicated objects that the Egyptians made. We know much about their construction from the survival of a complete, full-size ship buried in a pit beside the Great Pyramid at Giza around 2570 BC. The hull was made from carefully shaped timbers attached to wooden cross frames. Even when very large the timbers were held together with ropes and knots rather than with nails or other metal fastenings. The hull followed a distinctive curving line that raised the ends out of the water and tapered into tall points swelled into the shape of an open lotus flower. The steering of the boat was entrusted to long paddles lashed into a near-vertical position. A horizontal handle rotated the paddle which steered the boat like a rudder. Large boats had a pair of them, one on either side at the stern.

The unusually long Spell 99 introduces what at first sight is similar to the 'ferry-boat' of Greek mythology, in which the dead had to cross the Styx to reach the land of the dead. For the ancient Egyptians the destination is the east, the place of sunrise, that lay across the river from the normal abode of the dead in the west. The first part of the spell records a dialogue in which the reader commands the attention of the boatman (Aqen) and his assistant (Mahaf). The early reference to Horus, restored to wholeness as the eye of a falcon (having had his eye torn from his head by Seth in revenge for his castration), prefigures the task of assembling the boat from its pieces. The dialogue develops into a display of scribal knowledge of the names of things – the parts of the boat are named and details of their assemblage. Each part of the boat is identified not only by its common name but by its personal, magical name. For the Egyptian, knowledge is power. The name of something is one of its essential properties.

At the end of the list, that extends to include the secret names of the captain, the wind, the river, the banks of the river and the ground, the reader addresses them all. His success in commanding the boat − and their assent − is signified by the funeral meal presented to him:

> Hail to you, you whose natures are kind, possessors of offerings who live forever and ever! I have penetrated to you so that you may give me a funeral meal for my mouth with which I speak, namely the cake which Isis baked in the presence of the Great God to whose nose you present provisions, whose name is Tjekem. He reveals himself in the eastern horizon of the sky, he travels in the western horizon of the sky. When he departs, I will depart; when he is hale, I will be hale.

For a people so dependent upon a major river for transport the prominence of boat imagery is understandable. In the Otherworld, however, voyaging was for the sun-god and his companions. For the constant journeyings referred to in the Book of the Dead the means of transport is not generally mentioned, but the implication is that it was on foot. Many spells speak of pathways to be opened.

> *Spell for going out into the day after opening the tomb.* O you soul, greatly majestic, behold, I have come that I may see you; I open the Otherworld that I may see my father Osiris and drive away darkness, for I am beloved of him. I have come that I may see my father Osiris and that I may cut out the heart of Seth who has harmed my father Osiris. I have opened up every path which is in the sky and on earth, for I am the well-beloved son of my father Osiris. I am noble, I am a spirit, I am equipped; O all you gods and all you spirits, prepare a path for me. (Spell 9)

Spell 9 visualizes a journey from within the tomb – and from within the Otherworld – undertaken by the disembodied consciousness of the deceased to the daytime realm near the tomb where he will see his own soul and the god Osiris, who is here more or less identical with the soul, and will 'drive away darkness'. 'Darkness' in the Egyptian language meant more than the absence of light at night-time. Darkness was one of the four original properties from which the universe was created and so had the additional sense of non-existence.

An Egyptian's relations with the gods were based on give and take. Mostly the giving took the form of presenting an offering at a shrine in the hope or expectation that the god would do something good in return. In the larger temples this was institutionalized so that the source of offerings was often tracts of farmland donated as an act of piety, from which the fruits of the harvest would be presented to the divine images within the temples. In Spell 9 the speaker performs a service for Osiris as his donation, in which the speaker momentarily has the role of Horus and takes revenge on Seth. With this generous act the speaker's own status is enhanced – he becomes 'equipped' – and so the gods and spirits give him freedom to move anywhere, in the sky and on earth.

Here begin praises and recitations, going in and out of the realm of the dead, having benefit in the beautiful West, being in the suite of Osiris, resting at the food-table of Wennefer, going out into the day, taking any shape in which he desires to be, playing at draughts, sitting in a booth, and going forth as a living soul by the Osiris reader after he has died. (Spell 17)

Spell for going in and out of the West. To me belong all men, I have given everything to myself. I have gone in as a falcon, I have come out as a phoenix, the god who worships Ra. Prepare a path for me, that I may enter in peace into the beautiful West, for I belong to the Lake of Horus, I leash the hounds of Horus. Prepare a way for me, that I may go in and worship Osiris, the Lord of Life. (Spell 13)

The normal abode for the soul was in the vicinity of the tomb, although the setting is not described. In Spell 17 the deceased has the power to change shape, one of those shapes being that of a 'living soul'. The Egyptian word translated as soul is *ba*. Its shape was a bird with a human head. During a person's life it was like an inner companion, open to a dialogue with one's own self and acting as one's conscience. It was nurtured by living righteously and by being fed wisdom. Some of the most powerful gods possessed one or more *bas* of their own. After a person's death the *ba* lived on as one embodiment of the person's self, keeping close to the body. One Book of the Dead illustration (belonging to a man named Neb-ked) showed a cross-section through a tomb. The *ba*-bird descends the vertical shaft from the tomb chapel at ground level, its doorway still open, towards the burial chamber where the mummified corpse lies surrounded by its burial furniture.[11]

The spirits of the dead could take other forms. Two of the spells in the Book (nos. 87 and 88) respectively enable the reader to take the form of a snake and a crocodile, in the latter case losing none of its aggressive and unpredictable character: 'I am a crocodile immersed in dread; I am a crocodile who takes by robbery.' Often a spirit would become a species of bird. Falcon and phoenix (in effect a heron) are cited in Spell 13. A swallow was another favourite. The transformation was not taken entirely literally, though. A 'Spell for being transformed into a swallow' (no. 86) is followed by a conventional text in which the speaker is clearly human: 'I go forth by day, I walk on foot, having at my disposal the course of the sunlight . . . Behold, I am come. I have overthrown my enemies on earth; my corpse, it is buried.' The many scenes of the countryside found in tombs give no hint that the birds that are part of the natural setting were also the souls of the deceased.

As well as leaving the tomb and the Otherworld to visit the world of the living in a chosen form, it was important to be able to move back again, to 'the beautiful West'. It was here that Osiris (for whom another name was Wennefer) was most typically encountered, sitting at the head of a company of spirits presiding over a table of food – that central feature of the life of gods, kings and people and, as noted above, a symbol of mutual contentment.

The ancient Egyptians devoted much effort and expense to making their tombs and to decorating them. In the tombs of the kings of the New Kingdom in the Valley of Kings at Thebes, the long passages that descend through the rock – sometimes through several levels – were decorated with detailed scenes of the Otherworld and of the night sky and with a myriad of demons and spiritual helpers. Space was devoted to the caverns and to the gateways, and to the conflict with the serpent Apep. Excerpts from the Book of the Dead were included. Other kinds of scene, that showed the king in the world of the living, are rare and of minor importance. A few ancient annotated plans of these tombs have survived and record the ancient Egyptians' names for the parts of the labyrinth.[12] The passages were labelled 'god's passages', while the external stepped ramp bore the name 'god's passage which is upon the sun's path'. 'The sanctuaries in which the gods of the west/east repose' were niches on either side of one of the passages; 'door-keeper's rooms' were another part; a 'hall of

hindering' was followed by 'another hall of repelling enemies' and then a 'hall of truth'. The burial chamber was the
'house of gold' or 'the hall in which one rests'. These underground halls, left in perpetual darkness once the burial had
taken place, imitated the imagined route of the sun-god from
dusk until dawn.

Outside the royal family even rich people did not have
tombs like these. Wealthier officials aimed for a tomb which
combined a secure underground burial chamber with a chapel
above ground that could be opened on occasions to allow for
the offering of food and prayers to the dead. Although the
burial chamber was rarely decorated, whenever possible the
chapel was carved and painted. The subject matter was a com-
promise, reflecting how the chapel remained accessible to the
visits of the living. Often the preferred subjects celebrated
the life of the tomb-owner mostly as he spent it with his
family, sometimes dining with them, sometimes out with
them at his country estate. Increasingly during the New
Kingdom, however, the balance shifted away from the family
and the world of the living towards scenes of the gods and of
the afterlife. Sections of the Book of the Dead appeared.
None the less the dominant theme in tomb design remained
the chapel where the spirits of the dead were served in
straightforward ways, through preserving their names and
status and through continued food offerings.

One of a tomb's most conspicuous features was its doorway.
Through this the soul could emerge and assume the form it
wished, and then return again to be with the body of its
owner. Yet the Book of the Dead did not develop the theme
of interaction with the world of the living. When the souls of
the dead fluttered forth from the doorways of their tombs,
where did they go and whom did they see? The spells do not

follow these journeys. The closest they come to visualizing indulgence in an earthly pastime is in Spell 17, which promises journeys into the daytime world in a transformed state, and playing draughts, a quiet thoughtful pastime and an interesting preference to other ways of relaxing – hunting, fishing and enjoying family banquets – and to other more adventurous possibilities. At the heart of ancient Egypt lay a yearning for quiet though comfortable stay-at-home simplicity.

For many Egyptians the idea that the spirits of the dead had an existence at their tombs was a very real one. They wrote letters addressed to specific dead relatives and left them at their tombs.[13] In these letters the dead are far from the empowered, glorified individuals that the Book of the Dead sometimes describes. All those powerful declarations that made a person equal to the gods are forgotten. The Book of the Dead provided no protection against the letter-writing of the living. The dead were as open to pleading and cajolery by offended relatives as they were in life. They faced an eternity of nagging. 'I shall contend at law with you . . . in the presence of the Ennead of the West . . . What did I do against you? I took you for a wife when I was young . . . I did not divorce you or upset you . . . ,' wrote an aggrieved widower to his dead wife, though without specifying what his grievance was.

Egyptians also believed that a veritable army of unnamed spirits moved through the settlements of the living, especially at night. They had the power to bring sickness and ill fortune and were often cited in magical texts intended to ward off misfortune. One protection against them at night were pottery figurines of cobras placed in the corners of rooms where people slept, over which a special spell was recited.[14] Spirits of the dead were blamed for the loss of cattle, for damage to the threshing floor and for uproar in the house.[15] In Spell 86 the reader himself faces unnamed enemies. Taking the innocuous form of a swallow, he strides forth into the day. 'Behold I am come,' are his words, 'I have overthrown my enemies on earth; my corpse, it is buried.' As aggressor, does the reader's own self become, from the point of view of the living, one of the malevolent dead against whom others will take magical counter-measures? Are individuals from his own community amongst his enemies? Ancient Egyptian sources do not try to reconcile this or other similar situations, conflicting in their underlying logic. The shifts in viewpoint seem not to have created inner tensions. The texts, whether the Book of the Dead or the spells used in the houses of the living, are written only from the immediate point of view of the reader, who is the victor in the battle that is about to commence.

5

REVIEWING ONE'S LIFE

What should be said when arriving at this Hall of Justice, purging the reader of all the evil which he has done, and beholding the faces of the gods.

Hail to you, great god, Lord of Justice! I have come to you, my lord, that you may bring me so that I may see your beauty, for I know you and I know your name, and I know the names of the forty-two gods of those who are with you in this Hall of Justice, who live on those who cherish evil and who gulp down their blood on that day of the reckoning of characters in the presence of Wennefer [an alternative name for Osiris].

Behold the double son of the Songstresses; Lord of Truth is your name. Behold, I have come to you. I have brought you truth [*maat*], I have repelled falsehood for you. I have not done falsehood against men . . . I have not deprived the orphan of his property, I have not done what the gods detest, I have not calumniated a servant to his master, I have not caused pain, I have not made hungry, I have not made to weep, I have not killed, I have not given the command to kill, I have not made suffering for anyone . . .

    'Come!' says Thoth. 'What have you come for?'
    'I have come here to report.'
    'What is your condition?'

'I am pure from evil. I have excluded myself from the quarrels of those who are now living. I am not among them.'

'To whom shall I announce you?'

'You shall announce me to Him whose roof is fire, whose walls are living uraei, the floor of whose house is the waters.'

'Who is he?'

'He is Osiris.'

'Proceed. Behold, you are announced. Your bread is the Sacred Eye [of Horus], your beer is the Sacred Eye. What goes forth at the voice for you upon earth is the Sacred Eye.' (Spell 125)

The most serious hurdle faced when entering the Otherworld was an examination of the reader's personal conduct over his or her lifetime, as described in Spell 125, when the reader meets the judgement of Osiris. The Egyptians had a clear picture of acceptable and unacceptable behaviour, towards other persons, social institutions and the gods. A good person avoided harming others, helped those less fortunate and dutifully made offerings to the gods. In another part of Spell 125 the reader addresses the gods of the hall of justice: 'I have done what men say and with which the gods are pleased. I have propitiated god with what he desires; I have given bread to the hungry, water to the thirsty, clothes to the naked and a boat to him who was boatless.' There was no declaration of religious belief, no test of faith. The existence and the nature of the gods were sufficiently self-evident not to require it. What counted was how you behaved and not what you believed.

To maintain standards of good conduct in Egyptian society, people needed to be taught how to behave. Respected figures (always male) wrote books of instruction, standard reading matter for Egyptians. They were collections of hints and tips on living a wholesome life. They promoted a secure, stable and ordered civil society in which power lay with 'officials',

men who held a place in the administrative system of Egypt
and attracted respect. The teachings combined guidelines on
social norms with ethical guidance, in a straightforward style
that told the reader what to do and what not to do. Scribes or
officials were advised to temper their authority by adopting a
modest and quiet manner, and a sense of responsibility
towards those of a lower status. Although there were references to god, and to the concept of truth and justice in the
universe (*maat*), the authority in these texts derived from the
author, a man from the scribal class. They were his words and
not the words of a god.

A papyrus text written in the later New Kingdom includes
a list of eight authors whose teachings were widely known, all
from times long past.[16] The writings of some have survived.
Ptahhetep is one, the author of a long and much-copied
manual of advice on conduct and morals. Another, Neferti,
wrote a lament about Egypt in disorder, saved by the coming
of a good and powerful ruler reinforcing the message that
peace and prosperity depended upon sound government and
acceptance of social norms. The papyrus text itself is a teaching, its lesson being that fame through authorship counted for
more in the long run than the building of monuments. Of
these eight long-dead authors the text says:

> The children of others are given to them to be heirs,
> As if [they were] their own children.
> They hid their magic from the masses,
> But it is read in their teachings.
> Death extinguished their names,
> But books made them remembered.

The list of eight was not exhaustive. It omitted the teachings
of two kings from the same past era (the father of King

Merikare of the First Intermediate Period was one, King Amenemhat I of the early Middle Kingdom was the other). It ignored a far more recent writer, the scribe Any who wrote probably in the early part of the New Kingdom. Perhaps the list reflected nothing more significant than the contents of the author's own library. In Egyptian society no single sage or author of a teaching came to dominate, and none attracted followers. There was no 'school' of Ptahhetep, to be compared or contrasted with that of Any. Compared to the vigorous debate of the ancient Greeks, Egyptians preferred respectful compilation of past wisdom, viewing all of it as having merit, something made easier because the teachers themselves did not set out distinctive rules for a way of living. Their teachings seem to have been admired more for their style.

In life, bad conduct was not necessarily defined by the breaking of a particular law, rather by it causing sufficient offence to provoke written accusations. A few specimens have survived. They cover injury to others including rape and adultery, large-scale thefts of temple grain, cursing with the king's name, and – in the case of a priest – going on duty in the temple before ritually purifying the body. Such accusations could lead to a court trial, whose punishments could be harsh. Seeking or facing judgement, from village tribunal or from the grand office of the vizier, was part of the experience of being an ancient Egyptian. Commonly the quarrel of Horus and Seth ended with a judgement from a tribunal of gods, and in the Otherworld a similar tribunal of gods sat in judgement over the spirits of the dead, presided over by Osiris in the role of 'Lord of Truth (or Justice)'. On death, the ancient Egyptian expected to be led into his presence to have his life assessed. The process was illustrated in the Book of the Dead by a picture of a tall pair of scales surmounted by a figure of a baboon, symbolizing the presence of Thoth, god of wisdom. The reader's heart is placed on one of the scale pans, and in the other stands an ostrich feather, symbol of *maat*, the concept of truth, order and justice. Another form of Thoth, an ibis-headed human, stands ready to write down the verdict, and not far away, squatting on its haunches, is a composite animal who will devour the heart that is weighed down with wrong-doing. We are not told whether a single departure from right was enough to tilt the balance.

Spell 125 describes the tribunal and rehearses the scene in the Otherworld. The reader approaches Osiris with humility and respect, yet not wholly without presumption. 'I know you, I know your name, I know the names of the forty-two gods' – referring to those gods who assist Osiris as assessors. Reciting the names of the gods would give the defendant an advantage.

The Book of the Dead takes for granted that the reader will have done some bad things. Spell 125 is intended to purge the reader 'of all the evil that he has done'. The Egyptian view allowed for two contrary streams of thought, one which denied that any wrongdoing had been committed and one which sought ways of avoiding punishment for the fact that it had. In this way ancient Egyptians escaped the dilemma posed by religions that demand a faultless life.

In Spell 14 the reader admits harbouring an evil which provokes Osiris to anger, and then makes an appeal for forgiveness, reinforced with the inevitable Egyptian gesture of respect to gain favour.

Spell for removing anger from the heart of the god. Hail to you, you who descend in power, chief of all secret matters! Behold, my word is

> spoken: so says the god who was angry with me. Wrong is washed away, and it falls immediately. O Lords of Justice, put an end to the evil harm which is in me. O you companions of the God of Justice, may this god be gracious to me, may my evil be removed for you. O Lord of Offerings, as mighty ruler, behold I have brought to you a propitiation-offering so that you may live on it and that I may live on it. Be gracious to me and remove all anger which is in your heart against me. (Spell 14)

Offerings are presented to Osiris, who transforms, for the moment, into the 'Lord of Offerings'. No magic is summoned or special knowledge displayed. The text is a simple plea, of the kind that in English is normally called a prayer.

Another way to avoid a negative judgement in the Otherworld was to deny acts of wrongdoing. A detailed list of denials forms the main substance of the lengthy Spell 125, from which we can deduce the Egyptian code of moral conduct. We might expect such a list to forbid certain actions, using the blunt future tense found, say, in the Ten Commandments. 'You shall not . . .' However, translations of the Egyptian code normally use the past tense: 'I have not . . .', leaving the impression that the truth has been deliberately suppressed, given the likelihood that any person will have committed some regrettable acts during the course of life. Even the most exemplary person might hesitate over the statement 'I have not been neglectful'. Unlike a Catholic's confession, say, the Egyptians seem to have encouraged double standards when admitting fault, as is illustrated by Spell 30, intended to prevent the heart – the seat of consciousness – from speaking out against the reader's interests. 'My heart of my mother, my heart of my mother, my breast of my being, stand not against me as witness, oppose me not in the Council. Outweigh me not before the keeper of the balance.

You are my spirit that is in my body, Khnum who makes sound my limbs.' Thus muzzled, the way is clear for Thoth and Horus and the great company of Nine Gods (the Ennead), who sometimes sit in judgement to declare that the reader is innocent of wrongdoing, 'his deeds are righteous in the great balance, and no wrongdoing has been found in him'.

Egyptian verbal tenses do not fully mirror those of modern Western languages, however, and the form that is translated 'I have not' – e.g. 'I have not been deaf to words of truth' – is not confined to past actions. In reciting the wide range of specific acts of wrongdoing, through the denials, the reader was actually separating himself from these acts both in the past and in a continuous present.

The Egyptian moral code is mainly defined by the forty-two denials addressed individually to each of the forty-two gods of assessment by name. The offences listed are generically similar to those found in other societies throughout history: 'I have not robbed'; 'I have not killed men'; 'I have not destroyed food supplies'; 'I have not told lies'; 'I have not eavesdropped'; 'I have not been voluble in speech'; 'I have not reviled god'; 'I have not made distinctions for myself'. The ideal Egyptian citizen would be honest, kind and pious and dignified in manner.

A second list of thirty-six statements is also found in Spell 125 and contains more that is culturally specific: the assertion 'I have not daily made labour in excess of what was due to be done for me, my name has not reached the offices of those who control slaves' hinges on the Egyptian system of conscripted labour. 'I have not encroached upon fields' and 'I have not built a dam on flowing water' are codes for a society dependent upon irrigation agriculture where land-ownership was strictly defined. The list also covers irreligious behaviour:

'I have not lessened the food offerings in the temples, I have not destroyed the loaves of the gods, I have not taken away the food of the spirits' (presumably offerings left at private tombs); 'I have not trapped the birds from the preserves of the gods.' These denials and others like them reveal the strong Egyptian belief that a good relationship between humans and gods required regular nurture through payments in the form of food offerings. 'I have not opposed a god in his procession' probably refers to the Egyptian practice of carrying the portable image of a god in a festival procession. Sometimes the god would deviate from its expected course, singling out an individual or delivering an oracular answer to a question put to it.

The Book of the Dead contains a comprehensive code for right living, but Egyptologists today are divided over whether people read it. Maybe having the text buried beside one in the tomb was sufficient; reading the Book of the Dead could be postponed until death. But (as pointed out in Chapter 1) a few passages suggest that people read it during life, in part to secure freedom of movement for the spirit after death. 'As for him who knows this book on earth . . . , it is my word that he shall go out into the day in any shape that he desires' (Spell 72). More generally, however, the emphasis upon knowing the names of the beings of the Otherworld, which was so marked a feature of the Book of the Dead, must surely have encouraged people to read it and to commit its details to memory. The list of bad acts was a part of this, and so the Book of the Dead would have prodded the conscience of many an ancient Egyptian.

These sections also reveal how potent a figure Osiris was in ancient Egypt. He held the key to eternal life, and he would judge you on your daily behaviour following death. By the time the Book of the Dead was in widespread circulation – the period of the New Kingdom and later – maintaining the righteous path was a priority. To ensure the favour of Osiris, individuals added the phrase 'true of voice' (properly applied only after one had emerged successfully from the judgement of the dead) to their names, writing the phrase on the door-frames of their houses, and even, in formal contexts, prefacing their names with the term 'Osiris'.

Osiris possessed an important shrine at Abydos which drew pilgrims. Most towns and cities did not have shrines specially for Osiris, however, and continued to honour the local god or goddess of long historic association. This did not preclude popular expressions of devotion towards Osiris. In the later centuries of ancient Egyptian culture people donated bronze statuettes of divinities to their local temple, probably marking a special occasion in life. The statuette most frequently chosen depicted Osiris. Many thousands were found in the late nine-teenth century, in a huge collection of deliberately buried statues and statuettes in the temple at Karnak where the prime dedication of the building was to Amun-Ra. People did not respond so warmly to Amun-Ra, and there were far fewer statuettes of this god at Karnak and elsewhere. To judge from the numbers of bronze figures of Osiris found on archaeolog-ical sites throughout Egypt he was a truly national god.

Nevertheless, as far as we can see, taking seriously the claim to be 'true of voice' did not set individuals apart or limit their religious life to the cult of one particular god. People did not claim to be followers of Osiris rather than followers of another god. Nor did the Book of the Dead or any other Egyptian text ask you to do anything that designated you as a believer. Far from being asked to advertise your piety or adherence to a particular philosophy, you were encouraged to build upon self-restraint and fairly exercise such authority given you by society. For the ancient Egyptians religious belief was not a vehicle of conflict, but was part of society's homogeneous outlook.

6

THE BODY'S INTEGRITY

Spell for not letting the corpse perish. Now every mortal is thus, one who will die whether [men], herds, fowl, fish, snakes or worms; those who live will die. May no worm at all pass by; may they not come against me in their various shapes. You shall not give me over to that slayer who is in his lair, who kills the body, who rots the hidden one, who destroys a multitude of corpses, who lives by killing the living, who carries out his business and who does what has been commanded to him. You shall not give me over to his fingers, he shall not have power over me, for I am at your command, O Lord of the Gods.

Hail to you, my father Osiris! You shall possess your body; you shall not become corrupt, you shall not have worms, you shall not be distended, you shall not stink, you shall not become putrid, you shall not become worms. I am Khepri; I will possess my body forever, for I will not become corrupt, I will not decay, I will not be putrid, I will not become worms, I will not be faint because of the Eye of Shu, I exist, I am alive, I am strong, I have awaked in peace, I have not decayed, there is no destruction in my viscera, I have not been injured, my eye has not rotted, my skull has not been crushed, my ears are not deaf, my head has not removed itself from my neck, my tongue has not been taken away, my hair has not been cut off, my eyebrows have not been stripped, no injury has happened to me. My corpse is permanent, it will not perish nor be destroyed in this land forever. (Spell 154)

Spell for not permitting a man's heart to be taken from him in the realm of the dead. Hail to you, lords of eternity, founders of everlasting! Do not take the reader's heart with your fingers wherever his heart may be. You shall not raise any matter harmful to him, because as for this heart of the reader, this heart belongs to one whose names are great, whose words are mighty, who possesses his members. He sends out his heart which controls his body, his heart is announced to the gods, for the reader's heart is his own, he has power over it, and he will not say what he has done. (Spell 27)

The Egyptians held a horror of the indignities that the body was subject to after death. They knew that within a very short time a corpse began a complex and messy process of self-destruction, which affected all living beings, from people to worms. Burial in the ground removed the rotting body from view, but did not necessarily arrest the process. Spell 154 conveys the Egyptian fear and distaste at the body's fate after death. It imagines the processes of decay as not simply natural, brought about in part through the actions of 'worms', but as the work of an ungodly 'slayer' who works his fingers over the corpse.

The threat of decay even extended to the god Osiris, the one being who had most successfully triumphed over death. His body was still vulnerable to corruption, but in reciting Spell 181 the reader assisted Osiris in keeping his body intact: 'Your flesh is knit together for you, your members are recreated for you, your bones are reassembled for you'. And in helping Osiris, the reader defeated decay himself. In Spell 154 the reader adopts the identity of Khepri the 'becomer', a divine force that transforms the reader into a new state of existence once the reader rejects a catalogue of possible injuries. Reciting the spell, the body retained its proper physical, human shape in the Otherworld. Every single part of the body, even those most susceptible to rapid decay, such as eyes and viscera, were to survive unaltered. The power of words alone was enough to secure physical health after death, summed up by the firm statement in Spell 154: 'No injury has happened to me.' In Spell 10 particular stress is placed on the physicality of the body after death – physical health is as important as spiritual wellbeing after death: 'I have taken possession of the spirits of the great ones, because I am one who equips a myriad with my magic. I eat with my mouth, I defecate with my hinder-parts, for I am a god, lord of the Otherworld.'

The ideal of physical beauty is described in Spell 172: 'Your head, O my lord, is adorned with the tress of a woman of Asia; your face is brighter than the Mansion of the Moon; your upper part is lapis lazuli; your hair is blacker than all the doors of the Otherworld on the day of darkness, your hair is bestrewn with lapis lazuli, the upper part of your face is as the shining of Ra; your visage is covered with gold, and Horus has inlaid it with lapis lazuli.' This is how a god would appear in the Otherworld.

Despite the optimism about the power of such spells, from an early date in their history the Egyptians guarded against the worst aspects of the natural decay of the human body after death by the process of artificial mummification. Egyptians observed that bodies buried in dry desert locations shrivelled through rapid loss of moisture, but did not decompose. Brittle, reduced in volume and discoloured, they nevertheless retained much of their human shape. Artificial mummification was made possible with the discovery, at an early but unrecorded moment, that a salty, white crystalline substance found in the desert – natron –dried the flesh of muscle tissue.

The art of mummification developed slowly. At its most developed stage, the brain was extracted bit by bit after puncturing the thin bony plate at the upper end of the nasal passage, and the viscera were pulled out through a slit in the side of the body cavity. With almost apologetic respect, a metal plate in the shape of the magically protective Eye of Horus would be placed over the wound. Once removed, the viscera were mummified separately and buried in a set of four jars (the modern term is Canopic jars), generally each one under the protection of the sons of Horus: Imsety (of human form) for the liver, Hapy (baboon) for the lungs, Kebeh-senuef (falcon) for the intestines, and Duamutef (jackal) for the stomach. A text naming the particular god was written in hieroglyphs on the outside of each, and the lid of the jar was fashioned in the shape of the relevant god's head (human, baboon, falcon and jackal). The sons of Horus appear in the Book of the Dead, in Spell 151, but responsible for the body generally rather than for its inner parts. Each is given a short speech, for example, Kebeh-senuef: 'I join your bones together for you, I collect your members for you, I bring your heart to you, I set it in its place for you.' The sons of Horus were, in turn, under the protection of four goddesses, respectively Isis, Nephthys, Selkis and Neith, the texts on the Canopic jars stating that each of the sons was 'inside' his particular goddess.

Once the internal organs had been collected, natron was heaped onto the torso and limbs, drying out the body. To compensate for its emaciated appearance, the body was swathed in sheets and strips of linen. This was the appearance given to the god Osiris, who is always shown tightly wrapped in linen from feet to neck, although his head remained outside the covering as did his hands, left free to grasp his symbols of office (the crook and flail).

The removed brain was expendable, deemed an inert filler

to the skull, without a function that was vital to life. It needed no divine protector. For the Egyptians, the home of consciousness was located not in the brain but in the heart, for them the controlling force within the body. In Spell 27 the reader begs of the gods that they leave his heart in place. The spell also alludes to the independent character of the heart, which might give a man away. When the reader entered the hall of Osiris to be judged on his life's deeds, he had to assert his own authority over his heart so that it does 'not say what he has done' (that is, testify to his bad deeds). Because of its importance the heart, too, was removed during mummification, but was then, ideally, returned to the body cavity before the bandaging.

The full (and labour-intensive) process of mummification was a complex rite, through which grieving relatives could show their respect for the dead. For most people, though, the process was simply too expensive. Poorer Egyptians had to trust to the natural preservative qualities of the ground, especially the dry desert, and to the power of the spells of the Book of the Dead (assuming they had access to a copy). The proportion of people who could afford mummification is now hard to tell. Various factors make an assessment difficult. One is tomb robbery, ancient and modern, but of greater impact are natural process of destruction. Not all cemeteries were in the desert, especially those of communities who lived in the Nile delta. Burial was frequently in earth that was damp, so that only bones survive and even then not in a robust condition. On desert sites termite colonies have often eaten away tissue and cloth, again leaving little more than bones. It could be that only the families of people holding official positions could afford the process. A generous estimate is a figure of around 10 per cent of the population. The great majority of the ancient Egyptian dead would not, therefore, have been mummified, but quickly buried perhaps just wrapped in cloth.

The Book of the Dead did not devote much space to mummification. It is briefly alluded to: 'May it [the soul] see my corpse, may it rest on my mummy, which will never be destroyed or perish' (Spell 89); 'May [the god] Anubis embalm you' (Spell 172); but in the many illustrations found in a good copy of the Book, the body more often appears in its natural living state, even though the proper image of Osiris – with whom the owner sought identification – was mummified. Illustrations might show, instead, the reader as a young adult in the clothes of the living. In a well-known example of the Book in the British Museum, that belonged to the official Any, he is shown with his wife Tutu dressed in the billowing draped clothes that were the height of fashion in his time. Both wear heavy wigs, and Tutu has lotus flowers woven into hers.

The Book of the Dead concentrated on the dangers that decay could wreak on the body and the threats in the spiritual world, ignoring entirely the threat to the dead from tomb robbers impelled by greed. Archaeologists have found evidence that this took place in ancient Egyptian times, sometimes shortly after burial. If burials were in the sand of the desert, the robbers dug down until they located a head, then used the head as a means of dragging as much of the rest of the body as was firmly attached up on to the surface. In the process, arms and legs were left behind in the ground, and skulls were scattered.[17] Extensive records have survived from the trials of tomb robbers of the royal family at Thebes, dated towards the end of the New Kingdom (the decades following c. 1125 BC). One thief confessed to habitual robbery and to the bribery he used to escape from the official guardians:

> We set off to commit robberies in the funerary monuments according
> to our habitual practice . . . Some days later the guardians of Thebes
> learned that we had committed robberies in the west. They arrested
> us, and they confined me in the seat of the governor of Thebes. I took
> the twenty *deben* of gold that had fallen to me as my share. I gave
> them to the scribe of the district of Tameniu, Khaemope; he freed
> me. I rejoined my companions and they repaid me a share. I returned
> to this practice of plundering in the tombs of the dignitaries and the
> men of the land who lie in the west of Thebes, down to this day, along
> with other robbers who were with me, a large number of men of the
> land also dedicating themselves to pillage, group by group.[18]

In another account the robbers, who faced the gruesome
punishment of death by impaling, admitted setting fire to
what remained of the burial chamber of a king and his wife,
once they had robbed the tomb. In their own words:

> We opened their sarcophagi and their coffins, in which they were. We
> found the august mummy of this king provided with a sword, while a
> great number of amulets and gold jewels were on his neck, his mask
> on him, and that the venerable mummy of this king was entirely cov-
> ered with gold, his coffins accented with silver within and without
> and encrusted with every sort of august precious stone. We collected
> the gold that we found on this august mummy of this god, as well as
> the amulets and jewels which were on his neck and the coffins in
> which he rested. We found the royal wife in exactly the same condi-
> tion; we also collected everything we found on her. We set fire to their
> coffins; we took their accessories, which we found with them and
> which consisted of utensils of silver and bronze.[19]

The cemeteries of the poor did not escape the attentions of
robbers either, the robbers lured on by the hope that, one day,
they would be lucky and would hit upon a golden amulet.
Modern fiction has popularized the idea that curses against
robbers were written in tombs but this is not the case. The
few threats that were included in tomb inscriptions refer to

people who entered the tomb chapel in a state of impurity, the chapel having a degree of sanctity similar to that of a temple.

While families could not always protect the dead from robbers, where their wealth allowed, they could feed the spirits of their dead relatives. Regular offering ceremonies in the tomb chapel were paid for from an endowment that the tomb-owner had set up during his lifetime and which also supported the men whose job it was to guard the tombs of the necropolis. The offering ceremony was straightforward. A simple prayer was uttered in front of a statue of the tomb-owner, or at least a carved representation of a doorway behind which the deceased was thought to reside. Portions of food were laid out, water was poured, and then the food was collected up again for consumption by the person making the offering. Uttering the prayer was almost as good as presenting actual foodstuffs. 'It is a recital without expense,' stated the mayor of El-Kab, Paheri, in an address to the living carved in his tomb. 'I shall not fail to respond. The dead is father to him who acts for him. He does not forget him who libates for him. It is good for you to listen.'[20]

The ceremony in the tomb chapel was a copy of the standard temple ceremony, where the principal recipients were images of the gods. A well-placed individual in society might gain permission to erect a statue of him or herself within the temple, to receive a portion of the offerings already presented to the gods. Honoured individuals merged with the gods with apparent ease.

The labour of making the tomb, the work of mummification, and the subsequent provisions for an eternal memorial cult at the tomb were all practical aspects of death that, for a family of substance, was a major expenditure. Pictures of funerals painted in tombs show that burial was made into a public display of ritualized grief and mourning. The memory of the deceased was maintained through the perpetual cult at the tomb together with memorials to ancestors kept in houses. The living did their utmost for the dead, yet they imagined an ultimate destiny for them in the Otherworld over which they had no control other than through the spells of the Book of the Dead.

7

VOICE AND PERFORMANCE

Some of the spells of the Book of the Dead attempted to bridge the distance between the timeless Otherworld and the real world in which care for the dead through ritual was possible. In style and mythology they shared much with household texts used to alleviate illnesses and ward off malign spirits, as in this spell against plague:

> *Another [utterance], for warding off the breath of the vexation of the murderers and incendiaries, the emissaries of Sekhmet.* 'Retreat, murderers! No breeze will reach me so that those who sneak up would pass on, to rage against my face. I am Horus who passes along the wandering demons of Sekhmet. Horus, sprout of Sekhmet! I am the Unique One, the son of Bastet. I will not die on account of you!'
>
> Words to be said by a man with a staff of hard wood in his hand. Let him go outside and make a circle around his house. He will not die from the plague of the year.[21]

In this household spell against plague there is a clear relationship between author and reader. Someone skilled in healing has, at some time in the past, written down his knowledge. Another person, a healer, has acquired a copy and will follow the instructions at an appropriate moment in life, walking around the house making a circle with a wooden staff, all the while addressing – almost certainly aloud – the invisible spiritual forces that cause disease. As part of that address the healer identifies with the gods, much like those spells in the Book of the Dead.

As with the medical-magical texts for healing, several of the spells in the Book of the Dead provide instructions or promises delivered by an authorial voice that is external and addressed to the reader:

> As for him who shall recite this spell, it means prosperity on earth with Ra and a goodly burial with Osiris. (Spell 71)

> As for him who knows this spell, he shall not putrefy in Osiris's realm of the dead. (Spell 45)

> As for him who knows this book on earth or it is put in writing on the coffin, it is my word that he shall go out into the day in any shape that he desires . . . (Spell 72)

In the last case, the separation between writer and reader goes further. The spell promises the reader that physical proximity of the text to the deceased is enough. It is there to be read at any time in future eternity. The implication is that the deceased in the coffin is the reader, but envisaged in the mind of the living reader as his own future state. The reader is an actor in a ritual to benefit his own dead body:

> As for any noble dead for whom this ritual is performed over his coffin, there shall be opened for him four openings in the sky . . . No outsider knows, for it is a secret which the common folk do not yet know; you shall not perform it over anyone, not your father or your son, except yourself alone. It is truly a secret, which no one of the people should know. (Spell 161)

> The correct procedure in this Hall of Justice. One shall utter this spell pure and clean and clad in white garments and sandals, painted with black eye-paint and anointed with myrrh. There shall be offered to him meat and poultry . . . when you have put this written procedure on a clean floor of ochre overlaid with earth upon which no swine or small cattle have trodden. (Spell 125)

This is the moment when the reader, after death, faces the weighing of the heart in front of the tribunal of assessors. This part of the spell tells the reader, who elsewhere is concerned about the possible independent testimony of his heart, to perform a ritual as well, on a patch of clean floor.

The Book of the Dead revels in its shifting registers. The identity of the narrator's voice shifts between author to reader, alive and dead, and to the gods; and the boundary between the now of the living reader's experience of reading and imagining, and the visualized future existence after death, when the Book is still there to be read, is fluid. The complexity of who is speaking, and when, is magnified when individual passages are held up to close scrutiny, but when the spells are read as a single flow of words the shifts in perspective are less visible and the texts make reasonable sense, as they clearly must have done to the Egyptians.

Of the 176 spells in one of the standard modern collections, twenty-two (one eighth) include a specific instruction as to an action to take at the time of uttering the spell or, in the case of Spell 30, the instruction is actually to a craftsman who will make a particular object. The spells demanded that the reader perform rituals over objects that would then be placed on or around the body of the reader when deceased:

To be said over a golden *djed*-pillar [a tree-trunk-like object that stood for 'stability'] embellished with sycamore-bast, to be placed on the throat of the deceased on the day of interment. (Spell 155)

To be said over a knot-amulet of red jasper moistened with juice of the 'life-is-in-it' fruit and embellished with sycamore-bast and placed on the neck of the deceased on the day of interment. (Spell 156)

To be inscribed upon a scarab made from nephrite, mounted in fine gold, with a ring of silver, and placed at the throat of the deceased. (Spell 30)

The excavation by archaeologists of many tombs shows that when the time came to make a burial, appropriate objects were collected, some placed on the body, perhaps within the mummy wrappings, some placed around the body in the tomb chamber.[22] Some were utilitarian comforts for the after-life, some illustrated the symbolism of death and so were possibly objects over which the spells in the Book of the Dead were spoken. The objects and their arrangement vary considerably from tomb to tomb, and not necessarily in a way that reflects the wealth or status of the deceased. One has the impression that those responsible for the burial did not work from something like a shopping list, or visit an establishment where a ready-made burial kit could be purchased. Burial sets look more like a mixture of what happened to be available from the deceased person's own goods, and objects that friends and relatives donated out of goodwill. Thus a person might end up with more than one copy of the Book of the Dead.

In giving instructions about the placement of objects on the deceased, the Book of the Dead intrudes more obviously into the living world, and archaeologists can investigate how far people actually followed the directions. Unfortunately, so many tombs have been robbed that the number available for comparison are very few. One of them is the tomb, found in 1905 in the Valley of Kings, of Yuya and Tuyu, the father and mother of Tiy, the chief wife of king Amenhotep III. They evidently came from a wealthy provincial family and, as the king's father- and mother-in-law, were honoured with a burial in the place normally reserved for kings. Although they had their own sets of coffins, only Yuya was provided with a Book of the Dead (containing forty spells), and between them they mustered only seven amulets. One (a *djed*-pillar that illustrated Spell 155, see above) was not inscribed. The other six all bore the name of Tuyu, comprising another *djed*-pillar actually inscribed with Spell 155; three scarab amulets intended to illustrate Spell 30 but only one of them in a green stone; a red jasper knot-amulet of the kind that illustrated Spell 156; and a *ba*-bird of wood that might have been that referred to in Spell 89: 'To be spoken over a human-headed bird of gold inlaid with semi-precious stones and laid on the breast of the deceased', although there were no semi-precious stones in this one. The selection of spells contained in Yuya's copy of the Book of the Dead did not include numbers 30 and 89. Thus the husband had the Book of the Dead but not the amulets; his wife had the amulets but not the Book. The couple were most likely not buried at the same time. It seems that it was not necessary to follow very exact burial instructions.

One common burial object was a statuette of the deceased carrying a set of tools, inscribed with Spell 6. The statuette was intended to provide a substitute for the deceased if and when the call came for conscripted labour in the afterlife. An earlier version of the spell, found in the Coffin Texts, ends with the instruction that it should be spoken over an image of the deceased, made from particular kinds of wood and placed in the tomb chapel.[23] In its Book of the Dead rendering this instruction was dropped, and although wood continued to be one material used, other materials and especially a glazed composite substance, Egyptian faience – often bright blue or turquoise in colour – became common as well. Here we have a case where we know from the history and nature of the statuettes that one particular spell from the Book of the Dead had an object to accompany it, but this connection is not explicitly stated in the spell itself. Might the same disjointed relationship between text and practice apply to other spells and objects? Yuya and Tuyu's tomb contained eighteen beautifully made statuettes, fourteen naming Yuya and four Tuyu. Spell 6, although written on the statuettes, was not included in the forty spells chosen for Yuya's copy of the Book, an exact match again lacking between ritual object and what a particular copy of the Book of the Dead specified.

Yuya's Book of the Dead also contained two spells with the following instructions:

To be spoken by a man, when Ra manifests himself, over these gods depicted in paint on a writing-board. There shall be given to them offerings and provisions . . . It means that this soul will have provision in the realm of the dead; it means that a man will be saved from anything evil . . . and none of his enemies will know him in the realm of the dead, in the sky, on earth, or in any place where he may walk. (Spell 148)

To be spoken over four torches of red linen smeared with best quality Libyan oil in the hands of four men on whose arms are inscribed the names of the Children of Horus. They are to be lighted in broad daylight, in order to give this spirit power over the Imperishable Stars . . . Beware greatly lest you do this before anyone except yourself, with your father or your son, because it is a great secret of the

West, a secret image of the Otherworld, since the gods, spirits and
dead see it as the shape of the Foremost of the Westerners [i.e.
Osiris]. (Spell 137A)

Nothing in Yuya's tomb resembled the specified writing-
board or four torches of red linen. Was this an omission? One
possibility is that the rituals were not performed only in the
burial chamber. The recitation of Spell 134 over an elabo-
rately drawn image of a falcon is to be accompanied by an
offering of 'incense on the fire and roasted ducks' and a promise that 'he for whom this is done will voyage and be with Ra
every day'. Burial chambers were not places for rituals involving fire, and the promise suggests that the ritual should be
performed every day. Tombs normally had a chapel that could
be very close, or occasionally some distance from the tomb.
Some individuals, by donating a statue of themselves to the
local temple, also gained a place in the temple cult. It is possible the instructions found in these spells, involving more
elaborate objects and the performance of a ceremony, were
carried out in one of these places. The person addressed
would then be a priest, maybe the deceased's son.

So much that is in the Book of the Dead was held in the
imagination, however, that it is probably not necessary to
interpret all passages literally. Spell 133 demands 'a Sacred
Barque of four cubits' [2 metres] length made of pieces of
malachite, and having upon it the tribunal of the nomes';
Spell 163 was to be spoken over:

a snake with two legs, a sun-disc and two horns; over two Sacred
Eyes, each with two legs and wings. In the pupil of one is the figure
of Him whose arm is raised and a head of Bes with two plumes,
whose back is like a falcon's. In the pupil of the other is a figure of
Him whose arm is raised and a head of Neith with two plumes, whose

back is like a falcon's. Drawn in dried myrrh mixed with wine,
repeated with green stone of Upper Egypt and water from the well
west of Egypt on a green bandage with which all a man's limbs are
enveloped.

These sound like fantasy creations, and the final instructions
for Spell 163 seem to exclude a ritual that was performed
somewhere other than in the burial chamber.

During the long period of time that the Book of the Dead
was in use – over a millennium and a half – a profound change
of view came about as to what constituted a proper burial. For
the first few centuries (roughly the first half of the New
Kingdom) the ancient tradition still prevailed of burying
household goods with the dead, from beds and mirrors to
musical instruments and pottery jars. By the end of the New
Kingdom this custom had faded out. The dead were now
accompanied only by amulets and other items that had specific
powers to protect the dead and enhance their well-being.
The Book of the Dead came to dictate what was proper for a
burial. Burial customs became more consistent in their outlook, moving closer to the prescriptions in the Book but not,
as far as one can see, using it as a detailed guide. There is no
evidence (even in later royal tombs) that anyone ever made a
malachite barque four cubits long. The increasing consistency
appears also in the contents of individual copies of the Book.
Whereas earlier versions tend to contain unpredictable selections and orderings of spells, in the later centuries a fairly
standardized content was preferred. It is on these later versions
that the modern numbering of the spells is based.

The Book of the Dead evokes a world of the imagination in
which the reader's individuality, and sense of time and place,
lost their boundaries. But despite its creative imaginings, the

Book also reflects the limitations of the ancient Egyptians. Learned people compiled the spells, sometimes composed additions and occasionally inserted explanatory comments, but neither they nor their readers thought to put into writing any reflections on what the Book of the Dead meant to them. This is true across the range of Egyptian literature. Egyptians seem to have entered into a particular text or genre of text and then, having exited, to have switched off from the experience. The Book of the Dead is a kind of fossil in the history of the human mind. It belongs to a people with a different sense of experience, knowledge and learning than we possess today. This is perhaps its greatest value. It preserves a mindset that is no longer living.

8

EMPOWERMENT

Spell for going out into the day. 'May I have power in my heart, may I have power in my arms, may I have power in my legs, may I have power in my mouth, may I have power in all my members, may I have power over invocation-offerings, may I have power over water . . . air . . . the waters . . . streams . . . riparian lands . . . men who would harm me . . . women who would harm me in the realm of the dead . . . those who would give orders to harm me upon earth.' (Spell 68)

Spell for opening the mouth of the reader. '*My mouth is opened by* Ptah and what was on my mouth has been loosened by my local god. Thoth comes indeed, filled and equipped with magic, and the bonds of Seth which restricted my mouth have been loosened. Atum has warded them off and has cast away the restrictions of Seth. *My mouth is opened, my mouth is split open by* Shu with that iron harpoon of his with which he split open the mouths of the gods. I am Sekhmet, and I sit beside Her who is in the great wind of the sky; I am Orion the Great who dwells with the Souls of Heliopolis. *As for any magic spell or any words which may be uttered against me*, the gods *will rise up* against it, even the entire Ennead.' (Spell 23)

Spell for becoming an elder of the tribunal. 'I am Atum who made the sky and created what exists, who came forth from the earth, who created seed, Lord of All, who fashioned the gods, the Great God, the self-created, the Lord of Life, who made the Ennead to flourish.'

See, I have come to you pure, divine, possessing a spirit, mighty, besouled. I have brought to you a measure of incense and natron, that I might drive away slaver therewith from your mouths. I have come that I may remove the ill which is in your hearts, I have removed the evil which is on you. I have brought you what is good, I have raised up to you what is true. For I know you, I know your names, I know your forms which were unknown. I have come into being among you, I appear in glory as that god who eats men and lives on gods, I am mighty among you as that god who is uplifted on his standard, to whom the gods come in joy, at whom the goddesses exult when they see him.'

'I have come to you, having appeared as son of you all. I sit in my seat which is in the horizon, I receive offerings upon my altar, I drink wine in the evening. Those who are in joy come to me, praise is given to me by those who are in the horizon in this my rank of the Lord of All. I am exalted as this noble god who is in the Great Mansion. The gods rejoice when they see him among those who go forth happily on the body of the Lower Sky when his mother Nut has borne him.'
(Spell 79)

A complete, functioning, reconstituted body would still not ensure a happy eternal life beyond the grave. The Otherworld was not a comforting place, an idyllic world, a paradise. It was full of alarming beings and prospects, all needing to be mastered single-handedly by the reader. There was no kindly saviour waiting reassuringly to welcome the dead.

Spell 68 is a mantra of power for the helpless spirit, for when he first finds himself in the Otherworld. The reader takes control of himself and then of his environment. The reader claims power for his heart – the seat of consciousness and intelligence – followed by the moving parts of the body. Then the reader claims control over the food and drink offerings, available when the living utter a prayer in front of an offering-niche in the tomb chapel, preferably accompanied by actual quantities of food. The term 'invocation-offerings' is a translation of a phrase that means literally 'what comes forth through the voice': the words are enough to summon up the food and drink for the dead. The reader next takes authority over nature: air, water and agricultural land in the Nile valley. Finally comes the claim to power over any men or women who might seek to do harm in the realm of the dead or, acknowledging that the reader is actually a living person, 'upon earth'.

The effectiveness of this spell was bound up in the Egyptian belief that thought originated in the heart. From there it took its shape and gained its force, being uttered as words by the mouth. The source of those thoughts was the god Ptah, who presided over the heart and tongue. A later religious text (the Memphite Theology) explains:

> It is Ptah, the very great, who has given [life] to all the gods and their *kas,* through this heart and through this tongue . . . Thus heart and tongue rule over all the limbs in accordance with the teaching that he is in every body and he is in every mouth, of all the gods, all mankind, all cattle, all creeping things, whatever lives, thinking whatever he wishes and commanding whatever he wishes.'[24]

Spell 23 reinforces the intimate connection between the gods and the spoken spells of the Book of the Dead. Ptah opens the reader's mouth, reinforced by other divine powers in a temporary consortium. The first divinity invoked is 'my local god', a reference, often made, to the god who presided over one's home town and shrine or temple. At Memphis this would be Ptah himself, but in the Delta city of Buto, for example, it would be the cobra-goddess Wadjit. Presumably if one was a resident of the Egyptian colonial town of Buhen in Nubia it would be 'Horus lord of Buhen', the deity whom

the Egyptians invented as the patron of this distant place. Next
Thoth is called upon, whose special province was language,
script and knowledge (he was also the local god of the city of
Hermopolis in Middle Egypt), and finally Atum, who
embodied the principle of first creation.

The spell alludes briefly to the ceremony of 'Opening the
Mouth', central to a good funeral. One of a team of priests
recited from a special ritual text over the mummified body
(and also over statues of the dead). The mouth was touched
with a blade that, according to ancient custom, should be
made of iron. That, and the title of the ceremony itself, suggest that its purpose was to reopen the channel for the
animating process by which, in each individual person, activ-
ity followed from vocalized ideas. In the words of the
Memphite Theology, with the god Ptah as its model:

> Sight, hearing, breathing – they report to the heart, and it makes
> every understanding come forth. As to the tongue, it repeats what the
> heart has devised . . . For every word of the god came about through
> what the heart devised and the tongue commanded. Thus all the fac-
> ulties were made and all the qualities determined, and those that
> make all foods and all provisions, through this word.[25]

Grafted on to this ritual was a re-enactment of the Horus-
Seth struggle, for the leading priest acted as the son Horus
and, in one of the ritual episodes, defied his father's enemies.
In Spell 23 the iron (described as a 'harpoon'), is wielded by
another power in the universe, Shu. The reader identifies
with the goddess Sekhmet who is to be found in both hot
winds and pestilence and in the cold and distant constellation
Orion.

The passage ends with a powerful assertion, thwarting the
use of magic spells by anyone else against the reader. The

Egyptian word that we translate as 'magic' and the English word seem to have a very similar usage. Magic, either good or bad, was brought about by uttering a special formula, often over an unusual concoction or an object of striking appearance. In a story recorded in a papyrus of the Middle Kingdom, Papyrus Westcar, but set in the past at the court of Khufu, builder of the Great Pyramid, a magician shows his skill by re-uniting the severed head of an animal to its body, which then walks away.[26] This is magic as entertainment. Mostly, however, magic had a serious purpose. It lay at the centre of Egyptian medicine, sometimes reinforcing quite rational surgical procedures. Evil forces are addressed by both doctor and healer with words that invoke the same mythology as found in the Book of the Dead.

Magic could be turned against another person. In another episode in Papyrus Westcar a priest uses magic to animate a crocodile figurine made of wax which, thrown into a bathing lake, comes alive and seizes the priest's unfaithful wife.[27] Magic was used in a conspiracy to gain admission to the inner parts of the palace prior to an assassination attempt upon King Rameses III (1184–1153 BC). A judicial enquiry later reported on one of the conspirators:

> He began to make magical writings in order to disorganize and spread
> confusion, making 'gods' of wax and men to render human limbs
> weak, and to send them to Pabekkamen . . . and to the other great
> enemies, with these words: 'Take them in', and of course, they took
> them in.[28]

If an individual fell out with the regime he could be named an enemy of the state, and he would appear in a list of enemies written on figurines of bound human captives – the object of magic intended to destroy enemies. An ancient Egyptian felt perpetually at risk from the hostile magic of others.

Ancient Egypt had laws, passed from time to time by Pharaoh. Mostly, however, Egyptians looked to a system of patrician justice for the resolution of problems with others. They relied upon the community to uphold the established order. Maintaining a safe and orderly society was down to people of good position who were ideally reserved, benign and committed to the idea of justice for all. Such people – and all in authority were encouraged to aspire to this ideal – could judge disputes individually, but for important matters they formed a tribunal. The tribunal is a recurrent image in the Book of the Dead. As described in Chapter 5, in its principal manifestation it was composed of forty-two assessors, each one responsible for judging a particular form of wrongdoing. It was to this tribunal that the dead were answerable before being allowed to proceed to the presence of Osiris and an eternal life.

Spell 79 places the reader amongst those who comprise the tribunal. As so often, the text immediately asserts the ultimate claim of power: the reader *is* one of the great gods, in this case Atum, the Lord of All, whose spontaneous self-generation began the sequence of creation that led to the appearance of the gods and subsequently to the material universe. One could not go higher than this. From this uncompromising claim to authority, the reader addresses fellow gods with deference, to show them respect. The reader begins with describing the bringing of incense – which induces contentment – and natron, the sprinkling or imbibing of which purifies. The source of the gods' discontent is not stated, but it is likely that they are presiding over the conflict between Horus and Seth, the archetypical source of disturbance in the universe.

A reminder of the reader's authority is not far behind, with the words 'I know you, I know your names, I know your forms which were unknown.' For something to exist, it must have a name and a form, but anyone who possesses this knowledge can control it. As we saw in Chapter 3, many of the features that make up a kind of topography of the Otherworld – mounds, caverns, doors, gates, cities – have names that the reader should know in order to control them although often no specific threat is implied. The statement 'I appear in glory as that god who eats men and lives on gods' is not an admission of cannibalism but another way to express the gaining of power over them. The alternation between the giving and the receiving of respect, around which this text is constructed, is a common device in the Book of the Dead.

Spell 79 ends with the reader seated as the head of the divine tribunal with the rank of Atum, the Lord of All. As the sun-god he is then reborn from the womb of the goddess of the sky, Nut. Her arching body is the sky, her frontal skin the surface on which the stars rest and across which the boat of the sun-god glides each day.

Through its language the texts of the Book constantly project the reader into a central position of authority. Reader and god merge, to become a single empowered self. The spells are uttered with assertions that the reader's identity is that of the gods:

> I am Atum-Khepri who came into being of himself upon the lap of his mother Nut. (Spell 24)

> I am he who opened a door in the sky, who rules from his throne, who adjudges those who are born this day [allusion to Osiris]. (Spell 42)

> I am a Great One, the son of a Great One, I am a flame, the son of a flame. (Spell 43)

I am the horned bull who rules the sky, Lord of Celestial Appearings, the Great Illuminator who came forth from the heat, who harnessed the years. (Spell 53)

I am this Egg which is in the Great Cackler, I am the guardian of this great being who separates the earth from the sky. (Spell 54)

I am Osiris. (Spell 45)

I am the jackal of jackals, I am Shu who draws the air into the presence of the sunshine to the limits of the sky, to the limits of the earth. (Spell 55)

Another way of merging with the gods is through statements in which this is implied:

I have arisen from the Egg which is in the secret land. (Spell 22)

My name has been remembered in the Per-neser, on that night of reckoning the years and of counting the months. (Spell 25)

My cavern is opened, the spirits fall within the darkness. (Spell 44)

Through these words the individual draws into himself all the varied powers of the universe and in effect becomes not only a god but the universe itself. He is alone in making the transformation from human to god. Only in rare pictures where husband and wife are shown together does another individual appear. The texts of the Book do not describe a community of the dead, whether of kings, relatives or ancestors. In death one's companions are the divine beings of the Otherworld. There is no hint that these gods are reincarnations of other deceased persons, even friends or relatives. The Book of the Dead assumes that a separate Otherworld exists for each and every person.

Ancient Egyptians spent their lives in an ordered, hierarchical society. Ethical teachings and their system of reward and punishment encouraged them to feel loyal dependency on Pharaoh. Memorial inscriptions in their tombs emphasized their subservience and loyalty. Pharaoh had the rank of god, an incarnation of Horus and a 'son of Ra'. Temples and shrines were dedicated to him. However, death released Egyptians from this world of servile obligation to temporal power that claimed to be divine. The king and his ancestors had no place in the Otherworld of the individual. In the personal universe that the Book of the Dead visualized, the ultimate authority is the reader's inner thoughts and voice. The king had his own universe, too, but one essentially the same as everyone else's, without subjects to rule. In this sense the Book of the Dead is supremely humanistic. It promised every reader that they would become their own universe.

9

BECOMING A GOD

Spell for being the successor of Osiris. I am the Radiant One, brother of the Radiant Goddess, [namely] Osiris the brother of Isis. My son [Horus] and his mother Isis have saved me from my enemies who would harm me. Bonds are on their arms, their hands and their feet, because of what they have done evilly against me. I am Osiris, the first-born of the company of the gods, eldest of the gods, heir of my father Geb. I am Osiris, Lord of persons, alive of breast, strong of hinder-parts, stiff of phallus, who is within the boundary of the common folk.

I am Orion who treads his land, who precedes the stars of the sky who are on the body of my mother Nut, who conceived me at her desire and bore me at her will . . . (Spell 69)

I am Ra, continually praised. I am the knot of the god within the tamarisk-tree. If I am hale then will Ra be hale today.

My hair is Nun. My face is Ra. My eyes are Hathor. My ears are Wepwawet. My nose is 'She who presides over her lotus-leaf'. My lips are Anubis. My molars are Selket. My incisors are Isis the goddess. My arms are the ram, the lord of Mendes. My breast is Neith, Lady of Sais. My back is Seth. My phallus is Osiris. My muscles are the lords of Kheraha. My chest is 'He who is greatly majestic'. My belly and my spine are Sekhmet. My buttocks are the Eye of Horus. My thighs and my calves are Nut. My feet are Ptah. My toes are living falcons. There is no member of mine devoid of a god and Thoth is the protection of all my flesh.

I am the daily sun. I am not grasped by my arms, I am not gripped by my hands. There are no men, gods, spirits, dead men, patricians, common people, sun-folk or robbers who shall harm me. I go forth hale, one whose name is unknown. (Spell 42)

I have forced the sacred gates, I have passed by the House of Kemkem, the 'knot-of-Isis' amulet has laid her hands on me, and she has commended me to her sister the Accuser by her own mother the Destroyer, she has set me in the eastern sky in which Ra appears and in which Ra is daily exalted. I have appeared in glory, I have been initiated, I have been ennobled as a god, and they have put me on that sacred road on which Thoth travelled when he pacified the Combatants and proceeded to Pe so that he might come to Dep. (Spell 75)

I am the soul of Ra who issued from the Abyss, that soul of the god who created authority. Wrong-doing is my detestation, and I will not see it. I think about righteousness, and I live by it. I am Authority which will never perish in this my name of 'Soul'. I came into being of myself within the Abyss in this my name of Khepri, and I come into being in it daily. (Spell 85)

Although followers of the mystic tradition Sufism seek union with god, the broad view of Christianity and Islam is that there is a limitless distance between god and the individual. These religions encourage humility, a sense of one's own insignificance and worthlessness that makes the individual more acceptable to god.

The Egyptian approach was as far removed from Christianity and Islam as could be. The gods threatened, yet their powers were there to be claimed by the individual. Becoming a god did not require patience and self-sacrifice, initiation procedures or distance from the material world. The Egyptian could become the greatest of the gods by simply proclaiming this to be so. And association with the gods was not for the achievement of worldly ambitions, but to ensure survival against the many threats to the eternal existence of the soul.

Spell 69 makes the reader the 'successor' of Osiris, by which is meant his full and complete replacement. In this version of the myth, Osiris is the brother of Isis and the father of their son, Horus, and has already secured victory over his enemies. A different telling of the myth describes the conception of Horus taking place after the formal death of his father Osiris. Isis, in the shape of a falcon, hovered over the body of Osiris who was swathed in the wrappings of mummification, but which left his erect penis exposed so that Isis 'received the seed, bore the heir, raised the child in solitude, his abode unknown'.[29] This version accounts for the claim that the Osiris-reader is 'stiff of phallus'.

Having become Osiris, of course, the reader is in charge of the court of judgement and so, logically, ought to be able to guarantee a satisfactory verdict when the reader's heart is weighed in judgement. But that would not be to play the full game. Egyptians, while believing they could assist themselves by becoming gods, still felt the fear of the final judgement.

The gods have separate identities, but maintain an underlying oneness. In Spell 69, the reader having declared himself Osiris, he immediately also associates himself with the constellation Orion. The plurality of possibilities is taken further in Spell 42. The reader is now Ra, the other great power in the universe. The reader considers his individual body parts. One by one, he states that they are identical to a god. Nineteen body parts are listed, all of them externally visible and eight of them belonging to the head. It is a snatched, incomplete listing, including the all-important heart but missing the internal parts, even though in different contexts they had their own protective deities, the four sons of Horus. Some of the links between body parts and gods are reasonably clear. The dark waviness of hair conjures up the mysterious watery element (Nun) from which matter was created. The face is the disk of the sun (Ra); eyes were a prominent symbol of the goddess Hathor. The ears are associated with Wepwawet, a god who appears as a dog or jackal with pointed upright ears. The heavy perfume of the lotus flower was commonly enjoyed by thrusting the open flower close to one's nose. But would not the god Wepwawet, whose name means 'opener of the ways', have been more appropriate for the lips than the other dog or jackal god Anubis who was, in this spell, the god of the lips? In the list of body parts the names of gods are simply manifestations of a general divine power. In the words that end the list – 'there is no member of mine devoid of a god' – an equally valid alternative translation is 'there is no member of mine devoid of divinity'.

The reader reverts into his role as sun-god, able to free himself from his enemies. The Book asserts that only the reader knows the name of Ra, who is otherwise 'one whose name is unknown'. The list of the reader's enemies is quite revealing in its order. Mostly it comprises a list of human or human-like categories, living and dead. 'Gods' are there, inserted in second place, after 'men' (or 'people' or 'Egyptians', the word having all these meanings).

As sun-god, the reader has several tasks. One is to undertake the sun-god's daily journey, poetically described in Spell 75. Having forced a way to the eastern horizon, protected by a living amulet that derives its power from Isis, the reader travels a road taken already by Thoth when he was peacefully resolving the quarrel between Horus and Seth (the 'Combatants'). The sun-god ends his journey at the ancient northern capital of Egypt, the twin cities of Pe and Dep, home of the cobra-goddess Wadjit who protected and symbolized the kingship of Lower Egypt (a modern translation of a name for a mythical prehistoric kingdom that took in the Nile delta). In the division of Upper and Lower Egypt lay an ancient memory of civil strife. In one of their several manifestations, Horus and Seth stand for the two halves of the kingdom of Egypt. The orderly rule of Egypt by the king derived from an accord reached in the mythical past by Horus and Seth who had once disputed the kingship. To what extent the myth had descended from a time when a united kingdom of Egypt was emerging (in the century or so prior to 3000 BC), and reflected a real political conflict between two matched but opposing kingdoms is nowadays much debated.[30]

In Spell 85 the reader becomes the 'soul' of the sun-god, possessing authority to maintain order in the universe. Here order means right personal behaviour, *maat*, against which the reader's heart will be weighed at the time of judgement. There is again no perceived inconsistency in the reader being, elsewhere in the Book, faced with the uncertainty of personal judgement and simultaneously being the sun-god who, from the time of creation (in the Abyss in this instance), has been the promoter of righteousness. The prospect of being a god did not give the individual the authority to act against the common good of society. It was not a licence to do whatever one wanted. For righteousness was what sustained the gods. *Maat* was the food on which they lived. This is literally illustrated in Spell 65, in which the contrast is made between Ra ascending to the sky to live on truth, and the god Hapy (the spirit of the river Nile) descending into the waters to live on fish (even though fish sometimes have the connotation of evil, although Hapy is always benign).

The Christian idea that free will in humans is part of god's plan is one attempt to face up to a world full of imperfections. The disruptive role of mankind appears in Spell 175, already considered in Chapter 2: 'O Thoth, what is it that has come about through the Children of Nut? They have made war, they have raised up tumult, they have done wrong, they have created rebellion, they have done slaughter, they have created imprisonment, they have reduced what was great to what is little in all that we have made. Show greatness, O Thoth! – so says Atum.'

The rebellion of mankind against the sun-god, at a time when he ruled as a king on earth, is the subject of a separate myth portrayed in scenes that decorate some of the royal tombs in the Valley of Kings.[31] As punishment Ra sends out his fiery 'eye', a disembodied part of himself that now takes on the form of the goddess Hathor, whose mission is to destroy mankind. The text does not grapple with the problem of free will. Having been chosen as the agent of vengeance, and thirsty for more blood, Hathor is thwarted by a now regretful sun-god who covers the land with red-pigmented beer to trick her into drunkenness. The narrative moves on to explain how the sun-god withdraws from the world of humans. He escapes by ascending to the tranquillity of the sky on the back of a celestial cow, who is simultaneously an image of Hathor but also has the name of the sky-goddess Nut, the stars and the solar barque arranged along her cow's belly. In his remoteness, Ra will no longer be troubled by mankind and so, from the Egyptian point of view, the problem is solved.

This part of Spell 175 concludes with the reader (as Atum)

separating himself from the rebellious faction. He aids Thoth, bringing him his writing materials, which are the god's instruments of power, with the words: 'I am not among those who betray their secrets. No betrayal shall come about through me.' Given that the stated purpose of the spell was 'for not dying again', the story of mankind's rebellion presumably served only to reinforce the reader's worthiness by citing an evil from which he can separate himself.

Personal empowerment was the prime purpose of the Book of the Dead, and identification with god the ultimate way to achieve it. Adopting a god's identity was not limited to the dead. Healers, whether professional physician or village healer, took the same stance, using papyrus texts written for the purpose. A spell to counter scorpions illustrates how, in their style and content, they overlap with the Book of the Dead.

> Stand still, scorpion that has come forth from under the fundament, that has come forth from under me, that sets fire to the great tree under which Ra is sitting. If [you] bite: I am Osiris. If you take me along: I am Horus. I am the snake that came forth from Heliopolis, the enemy. As for a scorpion, that enemy, a mountain is what lies before you. You will not know how to pass it. The protection is a protection of Horus. [32]

This transformative power did not undermine the organized religion of ancient Egypt. The Egyptians had a well developed sense of propriety, and were respectful when dealing with the gods. It was essential that the gods retained their full aura of authority, otherwise there would be no point in claiming identity with them.

There was, however, an elasticity of what constituted divinity which made the transformation into gods easier. Egyptians worshipped their gods and lavished wealth and fine buildings on them, but the gods did not necessarily rank above all else. Around 1000 BC the scribe Amenemope of the 'House of Life' (a place of learning attached to temples) compiled an extensive word-list intended to define the Egyptian universe.[33] The word 'heaven' headed the list, next came 'sun', 'moon' and 'star', and eventually topographic elements of the Nile valley. Amenemope then moved to ranks and occupations of people. It is here, albeit at its head, that he wrote the words 'god', 'goddess', followed by 'male spirit', 'female spirit', 'king', 'queen', and on into the titles of officialdom, starting with 'vizier'.

The words 'god' and 'goddess' derived from the word for 'being divine'. Divinity was a quality that lay unseen yet permeated the visible world and the imagined Otherworld, in the manifestations of gods and goddesses. Gods were both sympathetic understanding figures, who could be approached through a statue in a shrine and a conceptualization of a ubiquitous transcendental power.

The boundary around divinity was loosely and generously drawn. It extended to 'saints', a small category of highly respected men (there are no known female examples) whose statues were placed in shrines and offered the same services as more conventional gods. A complete shrine dedicated to one saint, Hekaib, has been recovered through excavation at the ancient town of Elephantine. He was a leading figure in local society in the 6th Dynasty (*c.* 2200 BC).[34] Many decades later the governing family of Elephantine erected a shrine for him and added shrines containing statues of themselves. The shrine of Hekaib and his 'companions' served as the principal focus of organized religion at Elephantine for over two centuries.

Divinity even extended into a range of aspects of the

human self. A certain scribe named Amenemhat requests in his
tomb that these parts of himself will live on in the afterlife:
his spirit (*ka*), the memorial tablet at his tomb (through
which his name would be kept alive), his soul (*ba*), his destiny, his
life, his 'illumination', his body, his shadow, his place of origin,
his upbringing, his personal creator-god (Khnum), 'all his
modes of being'. Each and every one of them is described as
a 'god'.[35]

In the Egyptian mind divinity seems to embrace whatever
was animated, whatever was alive. Certain animals became
sacred, or were seen as the embodiments of named divinities:
the falcon for Horus, the dog or jackal for Wepwawet and
Anubis, the cobra for Wadjit, the ibis for Thoth. But just as
humanity was not sacred when encountered on the battlefield,
the Egyptians showed no reluctance to eat meat, even that of
animals which, in specific contexts, were regarded as sacred,
such as the goose, emblem of Amun-Ra, and the cow, image
of the goddess Hathor.

Ancient Egyptian religion survived even when Egypt
became a province of the Roman Empire. Some Romans
mocked what they found: 'You there, you dog-faced, linen-
vested Egyptian, who do you think you are, my good man,
and how do you consider yourself to be a god with that bark
of yours?' wrote the satirist Lucian in the second century
AD.[36] Later still, mockery turned into horror of idolatry as
Egyptian Christians showed their adherence to their faith by
smashing the images of the old gods and destroying their temples. In modern times ancient Egyptian religion has often
been seen as the epitome of a polytheism that was less enlight-
ened than the versions of monotheism that have become
so widespread in the world. The contrast does not, however,
lie only in belief in one god as against belief in many. It lies in

the language of spiritual power, the Egyptians using theirs with a greater flexibility than we are accustomed to. But pre-eminently the contrast lies in the distances that separate believers from their gods. For the ancient Egyptians god was remote and of many forms, and simultaneously a part of oneself.

PERPETUAL FEARS

Another spell for making a spirit worthy. Hail to him who dwells in his shrine, who rises and shines, who imprisons myriads at his will and who gives commands to the sun-folk, Khepri who dwells in his barque, for he has felled Apep. It is the children of Geb who will fell you, you enemies of the reader, who would demolish the Barque of Ra. Horus has cut off their heads in the sky like birds, and their goat-buttocks are in the Lake of Fish. As for any male or female adversary who would do harm to the reader, whether he is one who shall descend from the sky or ascend from the earth, who shall come by water or travel in company with the stars, Thoth the son of an eggshell who came out of the two eggshells shall decapitate them. Be dumb, be deaf before the reader! This is Ra, this god mightily terrible and greatly majestic; he will bathe in your blood, he will drink of your gore, O you who would do much harm to the reader in the barque of his father Ra. The reader is Horus; his mother Isis bore him, Nepthys nursed him, just as they did for Horus, in order to drive away the confederacy of Seth, and they see the Wereret-crown firm-planted on his head; they fall on their faces when the reader is triumphant over his enemies in the Upper Sky and the Lower Sky and in the tribunals of every god and every goddess. (Spell 134)

Spell for making provision for a spirit in the realm of the dead. O fathers of the gods and mothers of the gods who are over sky and earth and who are in the realm of the dead, save me from all kinds of harm and injury, from the trap with painful knives and from all things bad and harmful which may be said or done against me by men, gods, spirits of the dead, by day, by night, in the monthly festival, in the half-monthly festival, in the year or in what appertains to it. (Spell 148)

O Ra who are in your Egg, shining in your disc, rising in your horizon, swimming over your firmament, having no equal among the gods, sailing over the Supports of Shu, giving air with the breath of your mouth, illuminating the Two Lands with your sunshine, may you save me from that god whose shape is secret, whose eyebrows are the arms of the balance, on that night of reckoning up the robbers.

O Khepri in the midst of your Sacred Barque, primeval one whose body is eternity, save me from those who are in charge of those who are to be examined, to whom the Lord of All has given power to guard against his enemies, who put knives into the slaughter-houses, who do not leave their guardianship; their knives shall not cut into me, I shall not enter their slaughter-houses, I shall not fall victim to their slaughter-blocks, I shall not sit down on their fish-traps, no harm shall be done to me from those whom the gods detest. (Spell 17)

The great Red Crown has been given to me, and I go out into the day against that enemy of mine so that I might fetch him, for I have power over him. He has been given over to me and he shall not be taken from me, for an end will be put to him under me in the tribunal. I will eat him in the Great Field upon the altar of Wadjit, for I have power over him as Sekhmet the Great. (Spell 179)

The ancient Egyptian who bought the Book of the Dead could transform himself into the sun-god Ra, but in doing this, also took on the sun-god's enemies, amongst them the great serpent Apep. This creature appears briefly in the Book, in the passage cited from Spell 134, where it is quickly replaced first by the reader's own unspecified enemies and then by 'the

confederacy of Seth', a collective term for enemies to be encountered in the Otherworld. Spell 39 devotes a little more space to
Apep, who is cut with knives, decapitated and bound.

The Book of the Dead was only one amongst several compositions which depicted the Otherworld. They now have a
mixture of ancient and modern names and include the
Amduat ('What is in the Otherworld'), the Book of Gates, the
Book of Caverns and the Book of the Earth.[37] We know of
them primarily from copies painted on the interior walls of
the deep rock chambers and corridors of the tombs of the
kings of the New Kingdom in the Valley of Kings at Thebes.
In these versions illustrations of the Otherworld dominate
the texts. The central figure, the 'voice' of the reader, is now
the king. Perhaps because his supreme responsibility is to
maintain order and defeat chaos, enemies are given far more
attention. The great serpent Apep, immensely long and sinu-
ous, has a particularly prominent place, and seems more than
anything else to symbolize chaos. Apep attacks the sun-god as
he travels in the solar barque at night, passing the portals that
mark the hours of the night. The knife assaults on Apep provided the wall painters with an opportunity for vivid
delineation.

Also present in the Book of the Dead, as in these other
compositions, are enemies in human shape, who are (as Spell
17 above says) 'those whom the gods detest'. The reader of
Spell 65 (part of the purpose of which was 'to have power
over one's enemy') is anxious not to be counted amongst
them: 'I have never been in the confederacy of Seth.'
Association with the enemy was dangerous and might result in
being 'carried off as booty to Osiris', presumably to face terrible punishments. But mostly the fear is that the enemies will
directly attack the reader. Spells 17 and 148 reveal that the

sharpest fear is of knives; of being butchered, sometimes on a slaughter-block. This rather than burning haunted the Egyptian imagination.

Ancient Egyptian justice could dispense cruel punishments, although the details are not well documented. Some crimes carried the penalty of burning, some of impaling. Records from western Thebes during the later New Kingdom imply that cutting off of the nose and ears was a punishment often inflicted although, properly, it had to be sanctioned by Pharaoh. This punishment perhaps lies at the root of the Egyptians' fear of knives in the spells of the Book of the Dead, as it was a punishment that many Egyptians had witnessed. In Spell 179 knives become the reader's own weapons: 'I am a possessor of knives and I will not be robbed.'

The reader triumphs over his enemies by recourse to that familiar instrument of Egyptian justice, the tribunal, described in Spell 179. The loser's defeat was reinforced by the reader imagining that he will eat him, a not uncommon image of total power over another being.

In the other compositions, enemies and the cruel punishments they receive are given more detailed attention. They are made to walk upside down and to eat their own excrement; they are burnt or cooked and cut to pieces by butchers. Gods or demons feed on their entrails and drink their blood. The enemies of the sun-god are a significant force in the universe, their presence providing the chaos that opposed order and created the tension that the Egyptians felt instinctively pervaded the whole of existence. Enemies were not the same as the unrighteous who fail their test before Osiris. The unrighteous would be devoured immediately by a waiting monster, but not subject to the eternal punishments in Hell threatened by the Christianity of the Middle Ages, for example.

Spell 148, addressed to the full company of gods and goddesses, begs protection against harm from a long list of threats.
Men (and the word equally means 'Egyptians') head the list,
but are followed by gods and spirits of the dead. The danger
posed by the gods seems to lie in their unpredictable character. They cannot be fully controlled. Their inherent
contrariness is reflected in the wording of long spells that
were written out to protect young children against a whole
spectrum of dangers. The speakers, who are gods themselves,
promise (in this instance to an infant girl) that: 'We shall keep
her safe from . . . the gods who find someone in the country
and kill him [sic] in the town or vice versa. We shall keep her
safe from every god and every goddess who assumes manifestations when they are not appeased. We shall keep her safe
from the gods who seize someone instead of someone [else].'[38]
The Egyptians tried to cover every dangerous eventuality.

Although the Egyptians have had, since the time of the first
Greek visitors to Egypt, a reputation for being particularly
devout, religious scepticism could be quite profound. The
longest preserved account of the contest between Horus and
Seth is written, in a careful scribal hand, on a papyrus that was
part of a library built up by a scribal family who lived at the
ancient village of Deir el-Medina at Thebes.[39] Throughout
the narrative the gods display the weaknesses of humanity.
They quarrel, they sulk, they cheat and play practical jokes,
they insult one another with sarcasm. Near the end Osiris
writes a threatening letter to Ra, accusing the company of
gods of allowing Maat, the personification of righteousness,
to sink into the Otherworld and thus to lose her position of
influence. Speaking of his kingdom, which includes a place
of punishment, Osiris says to them, 'Where I live is full of savage-
looking messengers who fear no god or goddess. If I send

them out, they will bring me the heart of every evildoer, and they will be here with me.' The 'evildoers' are these unruly gods and goddesses. Their vulnerability is echoed in the words of a spell in the Book of the Dead (no. 124): 'As for any god or any goddess who shall oppose themselves to me, they shall be handed over to those who are in charge of the year, who live on hearts.' As with humans, so with gods: all contained the potential for good and evil. In life and death one had constantly to be on guard against enemies in both guises.

The story of Horus and Seth is especially illuminating. The gods behave like cantankerous colleagues in a bureaucratic administration, forming committees and writing letters. Apart from Seth in his quarrel with Horus, they do not rise to spectacular displays of naked anger by attacking one another with weapons or hostile magic. Instead they are a pathetic group of beings whom the author does not take seriously. The sun-god Ra is the butt of another story told as part of a healing spell for alleviating a scorpion sting.[40] As an old man Ra dribbles. Isis kneads his saliva into a clay serpent. As Ra strolls out to admire his creation, the serpent bites him. In agony, unable to cure himself, he is forced by Isis to reveal his secret name and, in return, she heals him (though without divulging the name to the readers of the papyrus).

The authors and readers of these stories are likely to have seen, perhaps every day, the monumental temples of Thebes which express vast confidence in the existence of great and worthy gods. The temple of Karnak is an impressive survivor. Yet it is likely that a proportion of Egyptians, at least, were adrift in a sea of mixed piety and scepticism. The Book of the Dead hovers between the fear that the gods are real and the demeaning assumption that they can be ordered around.

Egyptians expressed some of their hopes and fears about

their ultimate fate through song. The words of some songs performed at banquets were copied on to the walls of tombs. One urges the listener to enjoy life to the full, because no one really knows what happens after death: 'None comes from there to tell of their state, to tell of their needs, to calm our hearts, until we go where they have gone.'[41] Another song explicitly counters this, introducing its main theme with the words: 'I have heard those songs that are in the tombs of old, what they tell in extolling life on earth, in belittling the land of the dead.' It offers a very positive image of the West, the land of death: 'Strife is abhorrent to it; no one girds himself against his fellow; this land that has no opponent, all our kinsmen rest in it.'[42] Yet this is not at all the message of the Book of the Dead, where the reader, facing alone an eternity of threats, is far from everlasting peace. Perhaps the biggest fear of all was uncertainty itself.

Religion today is defined by belief. Faith has become an organizing principle for religion. It helps to make it more systematic, and it also helps people who do not believe to define themselves. The ancient Egyptians lived in a world where it was unnecessary for people to declare faith in gods and beliefs. These seem to have been accepted in the way that much science is today, with the crucial difference that the knowledge that people thought they had could not be demonstrated by logical deduction.

Some of the followers of current religions profess absolute belief in the tenets of their faith, raising the question of whether absolute belief itself has only developed as people have self-consciously defined their religions. In ancient Egypt one could offend society and be punished for acts of profane behaviour, in particular by entering a temple in a state of ritual uncleanliness. One could draw upon oneself the anger of a particular god or goddess and then seek to appease. But it is hard if not impossible to find evidence that in openly expressing disbelief or mocking the gods one tempted retribution from the living.

The Egyptians had created a complex and frightening spiritual world. Over the centuries they added ever more details and variations: caverns and gates, ways of torturing and destroying the enemies of the sun-god, and symbols of how the sun-god continually renewed his existence, a metaphor for personal renewal. Did any of it really exist? In the end they could neither know nor not know. They had not developed a theology: the concepts, the vocabulary and the argumentative skills to argue for or against their spiritual world and so to develop a level of unshakeable belief or absolute doubt. Hence the nervous, constantly shifting perspective of the Book of the Dead. It is an articulation of worry and uncertainty as much as of belief.

NOTES

1   In denying the secrecy of the text, and indeed in arguing that it was a basic part of a literate Egyptian's knowledge, I am disagreeing with the view that Egyptian religious knowledge was consciously restricted and that the gaining of this knowledge came about through initiation. Amongst those who have put forward this view are J. Baines ('Restricted knowledge, hierarchy, and decorum: modern perceptions and ancient institutions', *Journal of the American Research Center in Egypt* 27, 1990, 1–23) and J. Assmann (*Death and Salvation in Ancient Egypt*, Ithaca and London, Cornell University Press, 2005, 200–8). Although the evidence that counts remains extremely fragmentary for either position, I am impressed by the spread of texts of religious/magical content (some of which were to be spoken aloud in houses) and the archaeological evidence of amulets and figurines that in some cases seem to fit well the spirit world of the texts (the two references cited in note 14 are a good example). The ancient Egyptian words 'secret' and 'mysteries' belong, in my view, within a style of discourse in which qualities are mobile and only temporarily absolute. The intensity of detail in some of the texts that were placed in the tombs in the Valley of Kings probably made these texts self-restricting, in that most people would not have had the time or specialist interest to study them. But that is not the same thing.

2   The Book of the Dead Project based in the University of Bonn is developing an extensive archive and acts as a research centre. See www.uni-bonn.de/en/www/Book_of_the_Dead_Project/project. html. As the cataloguing of museum collections becomes more detailed, the numbers of known examples are going to increase. Some of the figures I quote for museum holdings are probably conservative.

3 C. M. Larson, *By His Own Hand upon Papyrus: A New Look at the Joseph Smith Papyri*, Grand Rapids, MI, Institute for Religious Research, 1992. Also the website: http://www.irr.org/MIT/Books/BHOH/bhoh2.html.

4 E. Hornung, *The Ancient Egyptian Books of the Afterlife*, translated by D. Lorton, Ithaca and London, Cornell University Press, 1999, p. 168, has a note on some of the wider interpretations of the Book of the Dead, including those of the theosophical movement.

5 T. M. Davis, G. Maspero, P. E. Newberry and H. Carter, *The Tomb of Iouiya and Touiyou*, London, Constable, 1907.

6 J. Gwyn Griffiths, *Plutarch's De Iside et Osiride*, Swansea, University of Wales Press, 1970.

7 L. H. Lesko, *The Ancient Egyptian Book of Two Ways*, Berkeley, Los Angeles and London, University of California Press, 1972.

8 J. A. Harrell and V. M. Brown, 'The oldest surviving topographical map from ancient Egypt (Turin Papyri 1879, 1899, and 1969)', *Journal of the American Research Center in Egypt* 29, 1992, pp. 81–105.

9 Papyrus Anastasi I, in E. Wente, *Letters from Ancient Egypt*, Atlanta, Scholars Press, 1990, pp. 106–9.

10 B. Landström, *Ships of the Pharaohs: 4000 Years of Egyptian Shipbuilding*, London, Allen and Unwin, 1970.

11 Illustrated in A. J. Spencer, *Death in Ancient Egypt*, Harmondsworth, Penguin, 1982, p. 59, Fig. 14.

12 C. Rossi, *Architecture and Mathematics in Ancient Egypt*, Cambridge, Cambridge University Press, 2004, pp. 140–7.

13 Wente, *Letters*, pp. 210–19, the quotation being from p. 216; A. G. McDowell, *Village Life in Ancient Egypt: Laundry Lists and Love Songs*. Oxford, Oxford University Press, 1999, pp. 106–7, no. 77.

14 R. K. Ritner, 'O. Gardiner 363: a spell against night terrors', *Journal of the American Research Center in Egypt* 27, 1990, pp. 25–41; K. Szpakowska, 'Playing with fire: initial observations on the religious uses of clay cobras from Amarna', *Journal of the American Research Center in Egypt* 40, 2003, pp. 113–22.

15 From the Teachings of Any, cited in McDowell, *Village Life*, p. 104.

16 Papyrus Chester Beatty IV, verso 2.5–3.11, translated in M. Lichtheim, *Ancient Egyptian Literature: A book of readings* II. *The*

New Kingdom, Berkeley, Los Angeles, London, University of California Press, 1976, pp. 175–8.

17 The example I have particularly in mind is a cemetery of poor people from Akhenaten's city of Tell el-Amarna (c. 1350 BC), currently being excavated under my direction by the Egypt Exploration Society.

18 Papyrus Leopold-Amherst II, 2.12–13.7, in P. Vernus, *Affairs and Scandals in Ancient Egypt,* translated from the French by D. Lorton, Ithaca and London, Cornell University Press, 2003, pp. 6–7.

19 Papyrus Leopold-Amherst II, 1.16–3.2, in Vernus, *Affairs and Scandals,* p. 40.

20 Lichtheim, *Literature* II, p. 20.

21 Papyrus Edwin Smith [50] 18, 11–16, in J. F. Borghouts, *Ancient Egyptian Magical Texts,* Leiden, Brill, 1978, p. 15, no. 15.

22 S. T. Smith, 'Intact tombs of the Seventeenth and Eighteenth Dynasties from Thebes and the New Kingdom burial system', *Mitteilungen des Deutschen Archäologischen Instituts Abteilung Kairo* 48, 1992, pp. 193–231.

23 Coffin Texts spell 472, in R. O. Faulkner, *The Ancient Egyptian Coffin Texts* II, Warminster, Aris and Phillips, 1977, pp. 106–7.

24 Lichtheim, *Literature* I, p. 54. The text is now regarded as having been composed much later than the Old Kingdom.

25 Lichtheim, *Literature* I, p. 54.

26 Lichtheim, *Literature* I, p. 219

27 W. K. Simpson, ed., *The Literature of Ancient Egypt: An Anthology of Stories, instructions, and poetry,* New Haven and London, Yale University Press, 1972, pp. 17–18.

28 Papyrus Rollin, in Vernus, *Affairs and Scandals,* p. 115.

29 J. Gwyn Griffiths, *The Conflict of Horus and Seth: From Egyptian and Classical Sources,* Liverpool, Liverpool University Press, 1960, p. 105.

30 B. J. Kemp, *Ancient Egypt: Anatomy of a Civilization,* 2nd revised edition, London and New York, Routledge, 2005, pp. 69–110; D. Wengrow, *The Archaeology of Early Egypt: Social Transformations in North-East Africa, 10,000 to 2650 BC,* Cambridge, Cambridge University Press, 2006.

31 E. Hornung, *The Ancient Egyptian Books of the Afterlife,* translated by

D. Lorton, Ithaca and London, Cornell University Press, 1999, pp. 148–51; A. Piankoff, *The Shrines of Tut-Ankh-Amon*, New York and Evanston, Harper and Row 1955, pp. 27–37.

32 Papyrus Turin 1993 [17], verso 5.4–6, in Borghouts, *Magical Texts*, p. 77, no. 106.

33 A. H. Gardiner, *Ancient Egyptian Onomastica*, London, Oxford University Press, 1947.

34 L. Habachi, *Elephantine* IV. *The sanctuary of Heqaib,* Mainz am Rhein, Von Zabern, 1985.

35 N. de G. Davies and A. H. Gardiner, *The Tomb of Amenemhet* (no. 82), London, Egypt Exploration Fund, 1915, pp. 99–100.

36 Quoted in A. K. Bowman, *Egypt after the Pharaohs: 332 BC–AD 642*, London, British Museum Publications, 1986, p. 178.

37 Summarized, with extensive bibliographies, in Hornung, *Books of the Afterlife*.

38 I. E. S Edwards, *Hieratic Papyri in the British Museum* IV. *Oracular amuletic decrees of the Late New Kingdom*, London, British Museum, 1960, pp. 4–5.

39 Papyrus Chester Beatty I, recto, in Lichtheim, *Literature* II, pp. 214–23.

40 J. B. Pritchard, ed., *Ancient Near Eastern Texts: Relating to the Old Testament*, Princeton, NJ, Princeton University Press, 1950, pp. 12–14.

41 Lichtheim, *Literature* I, p. 196.

42 Lichtheim, *Literature* II, pp. 115–6.

CHRONOLOGY

c. 3150 BC   First preserved hieroglyphs, on small labels in the tomb of a king buried (in tomb U-j) at Abydos.

c. 3000 BC   The beginning of the numbered dynasties of kings of ancient Egypt.

c. 2345 BC   First royal pyramid, of King Unas, to contain the Pyramid Texts, carved precursors (intended only for the king) to the funerary literature from which the Book of the Dead ultimately developed.

c. 2100 BC   First Coffin Texts, developed from the Pyramid Texts and for a time painted on the coffins of commoners. Many spells of the Book of the Dead are closely derived from them.

c. 1600 BC   Earliest spells of the Book of the Dead, on the coffin of Queen Menthuhotep, an ancestor of the kings of the New Kingdom.

c. 1550 BC   From this time onwards – the beginning of the New Kingdom – papyrus copies of the Book of the Dead were in use.

c. 600 BC   Approximate time when the length and order of spells became standardized.

c. 450 BC   The Greek writer Herodotus visited Egypt and later recorded and disseminated his impressions in his *Histories*.

332 BC   Alexander the Great conquered Egypt.

30 BC   Death of Cleopatra VII, after which time Egypt was a Roman province.

2nd century AD   Possibly the last copies of the Book of the Dead were produced. This is a particularly poorly documented aspect of its history.

3rd century AD   By this time the conversion of Egypt to Christianity was being seen as a threat by the Roman emperors.

313   By the Edict of Milan the Emperor Constantine recognized the right of the Christian church to exist in the Roman Empire. Christianity rapidly spread in Egypt at the expense of the ancient religion.

641   Arab conquest of Egypt by Amr Ibn el-As.

1798   Napoleon's invasion of Egypt encourages European interest in ancient Egypt. In 1799 Vivant Denon, a scholar attached to the expedition, describes being handed a papyrus from a mummy which was actually a copy of the Book of the Dead.

1805   J. Marc Cadet makes the first publication, on 18 plates, of a Book of the Dead, *Copie figurée d'un Roleau de Papyrus trouvé à Thèbes dans un Tombeau des Rois, accompagnée d'une notice descriptive*, Paris, Levrault.

1822   J. François Champollion announces the key to the decipherment of ancient Egyptian hieroglyphic writing, subsequently developed in his later publications, the most extensive after his death in 1832.

1842   C. R. Lepsius publishes the first major study of the Book of the Dead, begins the numbering of the spells or chapters, and brings the name 'Book of the Dead' into general circulation.

SUGGESTIONS FOR FURTHER READING

E. Hornung, *Altägyptische Jenseitsbücher*, Darmstadt, Wissenschaftliche Buchgesellschaft, 1997; *The Ancient Egyptian Books of the Afterlife*, translated by D. Lorton, Ithaca and London, Cornell University Press, 1999, contains an extensive bibliography of studies and translations of the Book of the Dead and of all other comparable ancient Egyptian texts, including the Pyramid Texts and Coffin Texts.

The website of the Book of the Dead Project based in the University of Bonn contains a list of its own publications, see www.uni-bonn.de/en/www/Book_of_the_Dead_Project/project.html

Historic Editions and Translations

C. R. Lepsius, *Das Todtenbuch der Ägypter, nach dem hieroglyphischen Papyrus in Turin*, Berlin, Nicolai, and Leipzig, Wigand, 1842. First pioneering edition which began the numbering of the spells or chapters. The Turin papyrus used belongs to the Ptolemaic Period.

E. Naville, *Das aegyptische Todtenbuch der XVIII bis XX Dynastie*, 3 vols, Berlin, Asher, 1886. A major complement to Lepsius's publication, based on 77 separate sources, all of them from the New Kingdom. Full facsimiles of texts.

E. A. Wallis Budge, *The Book of the Dead: The Papyrus of Ani in the British Museum*, London, British Museum 1895. Sumptuous colour facsimiles.

——, *The Book of the Dead: Facsimiles of the Papyri of Hunefer, Anhai, Kerasher and Netchemet with Supplementary Text from the Papyrus of Nu*, London, British Museum, 1899. More sumptuous colour facsimiles.

——, *The Book of the Dead: The Hieroglyphic Transcript and Translation into English of the Ancient Egyptian Papyrus of Ani.* First published by the British Museum in 1895, it remains oddly popular as a reprint and is still available from Gramercy Books, New York 1999. Its one advantage is the hieroglyphic transcript. The translations and discussion of Egyptian beliefs naturally reflect the state of scholarship of more than a century ago. Dover Books, New York, also reprinted a variant edition in 1967.

Current Editions

T. G. Allen, *The Egyptian Book of the Dead Documents in the Oriental Institute Museum at the University of Chicago*, Chicago, University of Chicago Press, 1960. Translations with notes and photographs of all sources.

――, *The Book of the Dead or Going Forth by Day: Ideas of the Ancient Egyptians concerning the Hereafter as Expressed in Their Own Terms*, Chicago, University of Chicago Press, 1974. A comprehensive set of translations with variants, and a table listing the equivalent spells in the earlier Coffin Texts and Pyramid Texts.

P. Barguet, *Le Livre des Morts des anciens Égyptiens*, Paris, Cerf, 1967. Introduction, translation and commentary.

R. O. Faulkner, *The Ancient Egyptian Book of the Dead*, translated by Raymond O. Faulkner, edited by Carol Andrews, London, British Museum Press, 1985. A handy set of translations illustrated with coloured photographs of several papyri in the British Museum.

M. Heerma Van Voss, *Zwischen Grab und Paradies*, Basel, Morf, 1971. Facsimile edition of a papyrus in the Leiden Museum.

M. Lichtheim, *Ancient Egyptian Literature: A Book of Readings* II. *The New Kingdom*, Berkeley, Los Angeles, London, University of California Press, 1976. Pages. 117–132 contain a selection of spells.

General Background

The Oxford History of Ancient Egypt, edited by Ian Shaw, Oxford, Oxford University Press, 2000. Readable, authoritative and well illustrated.

J. Baines and J. Malek, *Atlas of Ancient Egypt*, Oxford, Phaidon, 1980.

B. Manley, *The Penguin Historical Atlas of Ancient Egypt*, London, New York, etc., Penguin, 1996.

Egyptian Funerary Religion

The following is a small selection from an extensive literature on ancient Egyptian religion in which the Book of the Dead is frequently cited as a source.

J. P. Allen, J. Assmann, A. B. Lloyd, R. K. Ritner and D. P. Silverman, *Religion and Philosophy in Ancient Egypt*, New Haven, Yale University, 1989.

J. Assmann, *Tod und Jenseits im alten Ägypten*, Munich, Beck 2001; *Death and Salvation in Ancient Egypt*, translated by D. Lorton, Ithaca and London, Cornell University Press, 1999.

S. D'Auria, P. Lacovara and C.H. Roehrig, *Mummies and Magic: The Funerary Arts of Ancient Egypt*, Boston, Museum of Fine Arts, 1988.

A. Dodson, *The Canopic Equipment of the Kings of Egypt*, London, Kegan Paul International, 1994.

W. Grajetzki, *Burial Customs in Ancient Egypt: Life in Death for Rich and Poor*, London, Duckworth, 2003.

E. Hornung, *Altägyptische Jenseitsbücher*, Darmstadt, Wissenschaftliche Buchgesellschaft, 1997; *The Ancient Egyptian Books of the Afterlife*, translated by D. Lorton, Ithaca and London, Cornell University Press, 1999.

S. Ikram and A. Dodson, *The Mummy in Ancient Egypt: Equipping the Dead for Eternity*, London, Thames and Hudson, 1998.

C. N. Reeves and R. A. Wilkinson, *The Complete Valley of the Kings*, London, Thames and Hudson, 1996.

N. Reeves, *The Complete Tutankhamun*, London, Thames and Hudson, 1990.

R. K. Ritner, *The Mechanics of Ancient Egyptian Magical Practice*, Chicago, University of Chicago, Oriental Institute, 1993.

A. J. Spencer, *Death in Ancient Egypt*, Harmondsworth, Penguin, 1982.

J. H. Taylor, *Death and the Afterlife in Ancient Egypt*, London, British Museum Press, 2001.

R. Parkinson and S. Quirke, 'The coffin of prince Herunefer and the early history of the Book of the Dead,' In A. B. Lloyd, ed., *Studies in Pharaonic Religion and Society in Honour of J. Gwyn Griffiths*, London, Egypt Exploration Society, 1992. Pages 37–51 discuss the beginnings of the Book of the

INDEX

Places where passages are quoted from individual spells are printed in **bold** type.

INDEX

'voice' in the Book of the Dead
7, 18, 72, 74; in other books
102

Wadi Hammamat (place) 36
Wadjit (goddess) 83, 94, 98,
101
wax, images of 85
Wennefer (name of Osiris) 47,
49, 53
Wepwawet (god) 90, 93, 98

west, realm of the dead 8, 30,
40, 47, 48, 49, 78, 106;
Foremost of the Westerners
(Osiris) 78
wisdom literature, see
instructions, teachings
women as owners of Book of the
Dead 5

Yuya (father-in-law of king
Amenhotep III) 15, 76, 77, 78